# JUSTICE AS SANCTUARY

# JUSTICE AS SANCTUARY
## Toward a New System of Crime Control

Herman Bianchi

Indiana University Press

Bloomington and Indianapolis

The paper used in this publication meets the minimum
requirements of American National Standard for Information
Sciences—Permanence of Paper for Printed Library Materials,
ANSI Z39.48-1984.

♾™

Manufactured in the United States of America

Library of Congress Cataloging-in-Publication Data

Bianchi, H. (Herman), date
    Justice as sanctuary : toward a new system of crime control /
Herman Bianchi.
        p.    cm.
    Rev. version of: Gerechtigheid als vrijplaats. c1985.
    Includes bibliographical references and index.
    ISBN 0-253-31182-9 (cloth : alk. paper)
        1. Criminal justice, Administration of.    2. Dispute resolution
(Law)    3. Punishment in crime deterrence.    4. Victims of crimes.
I. Bianchi, H. (Herman), date    Gerechtigheid als vrijplaats.
II. Title.
K5001.B5    1994
345'.05—dc20
[342.55]                                                93-8386

1  2  3  4  5  98  97  96  95  94

# CONTENTS

# INTRODUCTION

NEARLY THIRTY YEARS ago I published *Ethiek van het straffen* (Ethics of punishing). The book was later translated from Dutch into German, and sections of it found their way into English translation in reviews. The greater part of the book was a discussion of the many arguments, stereotypes, and justifications advanced in favor of the punitive model of crime control, or what is generally known as modern criminal law. Such justifications have usually been based on Christian or false Christian doctrines. My principal and guiding idea was that if Christian doctrine has contributed so much to the rise of a system of crime control so unjust, malevolent, and ineffective as the present punitive system, we might also find in Christian doctrine the perspectives and concepts to get rid of that system. Such a method could be called homeopathic. Both Romano Guardini (1885–1968), the Italian-German scholar, and Jacques Maritain (1882–1973), the French philosopher, were fascinated by the idea of the homeopathic method, that is, healing the grave errors of Christian doctrine by conceptions derived from the same heritage.

To my surprise, though theologians were fond of the book and discussed it in many reviews, lawyers were less enthusiastic. I was disappointed, since, being a lawyer, I had written the book for my fellow lawyers and criminologists. I did not mind that theologians were discussing the innovative interpretations of Biblical principles, but theologians are not usually in a position, either socially or academically, to change the legal system. My intention had been to inspire change.

I soon recognized that the aversion many jurists had toward the book was right in some ways. It had been written somewhat prematurely. I never doubted that my opposition to the punitive system was justified, and I knew I was on the right track in laying bare the utterly mistaken religious arguments conventionally used in favor of it. But the question asked by some readers—"What are your alternatives?"—was valid. At that time I had no answer, other than stating that we had to find a more civil system of law. The direction we had to take was clear, but I was not yet able to present a comprehensive alternative. Still, a vital lesson—that it is not sufficient to point out the deficiencies of the system and its ideology, as so many people have done; it is also necessary to offer a new system to replace the old.

Since then, much has happened. Significant changes have taken place in the paradigms of the social sciences. In particular, criminology has gone through an important change. In the 1960s, progressive criminologists were as a rule still in favor of the medical model, which viewed criminal offenders as needing treatment by medical or psychotherapeutic means. Since 1968 a radical criminology has directed scholarly analysis to the prosecutors rather than the prosecuted. We began to realize that treating offenders as sick people is for the most part humiliating and beside the point, as it ignores the real problems. Since 1978 we have seen a revival of the idea of abolishing prisons. These abominable and unjust institutions do not effectively protect citizens from criminality but instead provoke new criminality by making inmates less fit to live in society than they had been before incarceration. It has been known for ages that prisons are superb schools for criminal education. They most certainly do not deter crime; they stigmatize offenders and are, economically speaking, a disaster. The frustrating part is that almost everyone has realized how wrong the prison system is, but it just goes on.

On the other hand, it would indeed be risky, even senseless, to abolish prisons while leaving the punitive crime-control system unchanged. For if the punitive authorities became convinced that prisons should be abolished—and the increasingly high cost of mass incarceration may well help convince them—they might be tempted to fall back on such once-popular kinds of punishment as forced labor, chain gangs, and the pillory. These "innovations" would, of course, likely be introduced under falsely humanizing guises, such as labor for public welfare, incapacitation, computer control, and the new pillory of enforced advertising and publication of ex-convicts' credentials in local newspapers. Why not reintroduce corporal punishment and call it behavior therapy?

People, including authorities, have a very short historical memory. They seem to forget that prisons were built to get rid of horrible types of physical and social punishment. But one punishment has been replaced by another, just as cruel. As long as the idea of punishment is kept intact as a reasonable reaction to crime, one cannot expect any good from a mere reform of the system. In short, we need a new and alternative system of crime control, no longer based on a punitive model but on different ethical and legal principles so that incarceration or any other kind of physical repression becomes for the most part unnecessary.

When, in my book on the ethics of punishing, I described the distorted Christian roots of the punitive model, I made an important discovery. If these same Christian principles, along with others from Biblical sources, were interpreted correctly, they would offer a remarkable body of sensitizing concepts useful in building a new model of crime control much more just than our present system. But I also made another discovery. If I were to use these Biblical principles, I might be running the risk of alienating the very people I hoped to reach. Would-be readers might confuse me with fundamentalist Protestants or Catholics who preach the idea of the infallibility of their own translations and interpretations of the Bible, answering everyone's problems with Biblical principles that must be accepted literally. Nothing could be further from my intention. For me, Biblical principles serve as sensitizing concepts and nothing more. I analyze Biblical principles not because the Bible is always right but because its principles are convenient concepts for gaining insights into our problem.

Whether we like it or not, our system of crime control has such deep roots in the ethical ground of our culture that an examination of religious thought is almost unavoidable. Crime control has generally been based on religious justifications of some kind; that being the case, it is much better to trace these religious concepts and use them for a better conception than to allow them to float in our unconscious, where they will do more harm than good.

But there is another risk in using Biblical concepts. Christian doctrine is the root of so much evil in the history of crime control that it is quite understandable that many people would prefer to clear the crime-control system of all traces of religious abuse.

They go so far as to regard with aversion any religious considerations in discussions of crime control, even being disinclined to take part in such discussions. This viewpoint is understandable, but it is not reasonable. Making conscious use of religious principles is better than ignoring them, given that crime control has always been based on religious beliefs of whatever creed. All humankind is, after all, *homo religiosus*.

Many scholars who favor reform of the repressive legal system show a distinct preference for the idea of humanization, going so far as to make it almost a religious principle. If we would just make the repression "humane," they think, everything would be much better; when inflicting pain we should try to inflict the minimum amount necessary to achieve the maximum results. They are mistaken. One cannot make a repressive system humane, just as war can never be made humane. The concept of humanization in itself does not offer a perspective for better law. Consequently, what I propose is not a humanizing reform of the present system of crime control. *This book presents a well-grounded draft for a nonpunitive but effective system of controlling criminality, based on conflict resolution.*

Discontent regarding the punitive system of crime control has been prevalent for quite some time. In particular the twentieth century has brought many proposals to reform or alter the system. Usually the proposals are intended to change the type of punishment while leaving the punitive system itself intact. Changing the type of punishment—that is, introducing so-called alternative punishment—might be a risky enterprise, leading to a worse situation. But attempts to describe a new nonpunitive system of crime control are equally risky if the proposals are not based on sound philosophical and theoretical principles.

The most basic concept of law is the idea of justice. Therefore I begin in the first chapter with a discussion of this idea. Being dissatisfied with the conventional concept, I propose another concept even more ancient than the famous Aristotelian one. What I call the *tsedeka model* is a common and universal concept in the legal system—except, strangely enough, in criminal law. This is why our present criminal law is in fact no law at all, not being based in the general justice idea. Other basic concepts, such as guilt and duty, repentance and reconciliation, are similarly discussed in chapter I.

Another important feature in this book is the use of historical and cross-time analysis. Changes in systems of crime control do not just appear out of the blue. History is important in order to check up on the right time for change.

In trying to describe an entirely different system of crime control, I have found it expedient to coin some new terms in order to prevent conventional thought from creeping in. To make a new system of conflict resolution stand out against the conventional punitive system, I introduce one such term, *eunomic*, in chapter 2. The present system of law is *anomic* or *alienating*, because it frustrates the main participants in a crime conflict, whereas its opposite, a *eunomic*, or *integrative*, system of law, offers both participants a way out.

The entire third chapter is given to a description of a eunomic system standing out against the present anomic one. And here I introduce another new concept. The common belief that our interpretations of norms and values need to be based on consensus is the sting in the present punitive system. It cannot but result in repression, nestled in the arrogance of power. To the *consensus model* I oppose the *assensus model*, which posits an unending, never-accomplished search for interpretations of norms and values.

The fourth chapter is dedicated to the question of how a eunomic assensus-based system of dispute settlement and conflict resolution can be implemented within our existing legal systems. It will be less difficult than one might think if we only drop the stereotyped idea of a crime-control system with structures and procedures different from all other parts of the legal system, such as civil, common, and labor law. Our peculiar mode of crime control developed because of its punitive basis. But if the obsession with punishment decreases, there is no longer any need for a different mode. The question also arises whether there is any need to continue the present state monopoly of crime control after a eunomic system is allowed to function.

One main obstacle to a nonpunitive system of crime control is the risk of popular self-help justice, such as lynching, in the case of violent crimes. In chapter 5 I discuss the idea of reintroducing sanctuaries to replace jails in order to make dispute settlement attainable in cases of very violent crimes.

In the final chapter I discuss the complex problems of politics and the practical feasibility of a eunomic crime-control system. A general survey is not possible because of the diversity of legal traditions and systems in various countries and even within the United States. Yet a few general remarks can be made with respect to how we may proceed in changing attitudes and structures with the least possible pain.

# JUSTICE AS SANCTUARY

# 1

# THE IDEA OF JUSTICE

SORCERERS AND MAGICIANS, shamans and philosophers, priests and rulers, authorities and lawyers have known since time immemorial that any good legislation must be based on a right notion of the meaning of justice. It is for this reason remarkable to note that after the Age of Enlightenment, discussions of the idea of justice became, until recently, nearly extinct in the West.

We Westerners apparently developed such confidence in the moral power and expertise of modern legislation as to assume that any law should in principle be considered good if properly handed down by a formal legislator. That is what we call legal positivism. It is odd, however, because great legislators in former periods as a rule set out on their enterprise by presenting a definition of what they understood by justice. The Byzantine emperor Justinian, for example, did it in the sixth century when compiling his famous civil code. In fact, his definition of justice is the first line of the first title of the first book. It is a good idea to follow his example.

But discussing the concept of justice is not just a return to a sound ancient custom. Today it is an obvious necessity. Any discussion of a crime-control system—the present one or something different—needs to be preceded by a fundamental explanatory discussion of the concept of justice.

Since the very beginning of the present system of crime control and more so in the nineteenth and twentieth centuries, criticism and complaints have been rife. Many proposals have been made to introduce reform. But all too often the critics make a fundamental mistake. They refrain from a discussion and explanation of the concept of justice. This failure leads to regrettable errors in thinking. Without even asking whether punishment—the hall-mark of the present system—belongs to a system of justice at all and assuming that punishment is a self-evident, necessary, almost natural and unavoidable type of crime control, they usually propose, out of the goodness of their heart, a softening of this repressive system. Their lack of philosophical reflection on the concept of justice usually makes the results they achieve practically nil or even the very contrary of what they intended.

It is not difficult to convince rulers and punitive authorities that new times need new types of punishment. Often they are the first to agree. They do not mind instituting new types of punishment so long as they can continue to punish and so long as their implicit idea of justice is not brought into discussion. The variety of possible punishments is, however, limited, mere variations on a theme. To avoid the real risk that authorities will fall back on ancient types of punishment in new guises, we need first and foremost to form an implicit idea of justice. Such a tool can be used not only to assess and reject the present system but also to conceive a new system of crime control.

There is one more reason for this insistence. Far from proposing a reform of the present repressive system, I argue for putting in place an entirely different system of crime control, a system that may seem novel but really is not, for it was in common use in former periods of our own culture and in cultures different from our own. It is a system far more consistent with the great concept of justice than our present punitive model has ever been. To look at it, we must pick up lines of crime control that were cut off during the Enlightenment, when the present system was imposed as a nostrum, making any other type of crime control illegal or at least obscure.

Let us first try to avoid some misunderstandings. Although this book is written by a scholar of law, history, and social sciences, not by a theologian, in these early pages the reader will find theological or Biblical references.[1] There are two reasons for this. First, as noted in the introduction, religion has had a preponderant influence on the origins of our punitive system of crime control, and I am using a homeopathic method to find the concepts needed to study strategies of change. Second, I have a particular interest in the logic of theological learning. This kind of logic still permeates our reasoning about crime control, although most penologists seem to be unaware of it. Ignorance of this logic is one of the reasons why critics of the punitive system often have had little success so far.

By no means do we critics assume that theological logic is better than, say, Aristotelian logic—or vice versa. Ignorance has negative consequences on any kind of logic. In the present case an awareness of the logic of theological learning is badly needed, not only for understanding the present punitive system but also for changing it.

Let me state once again, however, that I do not consider the Bible as some kind of supreme legal code demanding blind obedience because it is assumed to be revelation. I see its ethics rather as an invitation for discussion. Any religious concept in this book is used merely for sensitization.

## Law and Justice

In the best Western traditions it is common to consider justice as an ethical concept, an excellent notion at first sight but problematic if related to law.[2] Ethical principles often are easily formulated, without taking into account practical reality and feasibility or strategies of application. A concept such as justice, as it has often been proposed in ethical arguments, should be applied predominantly in the fields and rule systems of morality because its rules are better suited to that sort of highly raised principle. Law, it is argued, may operate quite well without ascribing a central function to ethical principles.

For several reasons we may reject such contradictory arguments. In the course of history, justice and law have always been conceived of together. In some languages the two words are even etymologically similar (in Latin, *ius* and *iustitia*; in Dutch and German, *Recht* and *Gerechtigheid*). In other languages they have different roots (French *droit* and *justice*, English *law* and *justice*). The English language moreover has a particular difficulty: *law* means both "law" (*droit* in French) and "the law" (*la loi* in French). It is all somewhat confusing in international usage. It may well be that this peculiarity of the English language stems from the rule of the Norman kings, who, from their subdued Anglo-Saxon subjects, accepted no discussion of whether *law* was the same as *droit* but simply imposed the king's law, calling it *the* law.

In non-Western cultures the matter of exclusive application of justice in the domain of ethics cannot possibly be raised. Only in Western culture do we find a philosophical and social development resulting in separation of the domains of law and ethics, the two being conceived of as different in nature and application. We Westerners have established systems of economics, law, social life, and personal life, state and individual, perceiving them side by side and assuming they are all based on different rules. In the history of our culture we can notice how again and again social life has been sacrificed to economic or technological needs, with no justification other than the argument that we are dealing with different systems, compatible only so far as duty admits. We have suffered, and still suffer, from this sort of dissociation, and it seems hard to learn from experience.

Both law and morality need to be governed by ethics; if they are not, abuse of law follows. An unfortunate example in Western culture that results from a lack of reflection on justice is the abuse of law stemming from the imposition of ideas extracted from morality, such as the repressive penalization of several kinds of sexual behavior. Such an abuse has been rare in other cultures and even in more ancient phases of our own culture.

Justice and law, in this book, simply cannot be conceived of as separate or different or antagonistic. Law is, rather, impossible without a well-conceived idea of justice. Justice is a legal concept as much as an ethical one; we should not distinguish between law and ethics. That sounds like a truism, but history tells another story.

How careful we must be in this regard in using the term *justice* may be inferred from this strange English expression: "These people have to be brought to justice." It is a most shameful abuse of the word *justice*, for what the expression really means is "They should be forced to suffer and if possible hanged." How, in any language, can such a beautiful term be debased so as to mean willful infliction of pain and harm?[3]

To clarify the connection between law and justice and make it a topic fit for discussion, we need an explanation of the meaning of both. What do we understand by *law*? It is simply a system of rules. But a similar definition may be brought forward regarding morals and many other aspects of our society. Rules of law are principles that regulate those relations between humans concerning problems of law. That sounds like circular reasoning, and so it is. It is usually a matter of tradition whether a problem is assigned to the domain of law or to the domain of morals or economics, or any other domain. Sometimes it is a matter of origin. Rules of law sometimes originate from laws, but this does not hold true for the entire domain of law. Many laws do not arise from law at all but from customs, perhaps authorized by law. An acceptable definition of *law* seems to be that it concerns rules enforceable by any authority, court or state, but many rules are merely obeyed because of consensus or agreement. Likewise, rules of morals or economics are also enforceable—if not by state or court, then by subtle means of power no less coercive.

And what about *justice*? Any definition I give now will be provisional, since this entire chapter is concerned with this question. Justice is a principle serving to assess rules of law and their just operation and eventually to assess whether their promised effect has been realized. If such a principle were not available, rules of law would be afloat. A principle of justice without rules is worthless.

These considerations should encounter little opposition, though many scholars and lawyers might argue that we can do without any concept of justice in legal practice. In this regard it speaks volumes how little discussion of the concept of justice takes place during legal training. That may be the result of a lack of consensus regarding the concept. Legal minds usually prefer silence, leaving discussion to the layman. Perhaps members of the legal profession believe that we should infer their ideas about justice from the way they administer the law. In that case an explanation seems needless. But this is a fallacy. It is, on the contrary, of the greatest importance to make unambiguously clear what it is one wants to achieve by the administration of law.

My intent in this book is to figure out quite clearly how crime should be met by a legal system and by what means the system's aims can be presented and achieved. The idea of justice is not only a means to assess existing law and its administration but even more so a means to construct legislation. It is justice that generates law and not law, justice. Without justice you cannot have law, not even unjust law.

## The Justice Model

The tsedeka model of justice is the leading principle of this book, and a comprehensive discussion of it will be found in a later section of this chapter. For the moment I will delay a clear definition of this concept, believing it better to follow a line of ascending, or inductive, discourse by first discussing its opposite. In making the tsedeka model stand out against the conventional concept of justice (if, indeed, there is any such concept in the mind of punitive controllers), the "new" model becomes much clearer. In this chapter so far I have used the term *justice* to indicate both the classical model and the tsedeka model. From now on this word will define only the former model.

The justice model, which originates in ancient philosophy, was stated by Aristotle in the classical formula "Give everyone his due," a formula subsequently adopted by the Romans.[4] Emperor Justinian used the formula as the opening words of his legislation. Nonetheless, the formula is a rather fishy expedient to serve the legal process, for it is hard to know and always disputable what everyone's due is. The formula is not far from being a truism and could pave the road to a malicious kind of conservatism, since everyone will consider his due to be all that he always had, permanent property being the best way to prove what is one's due.

Even more dubious is another frame in which the formula is often couched: "Justice is the constant intention to give everyone his due." Never is it said, "See to it that everyone really gets his due!" No, the constant intention apparently suffices; the result of the act of intention is not worth mentioning.[5] As Ovid suggests, "though strength may fail, intention should be praised."[6] Such primacy of intention was a feature of ancient philosophy and has forever remained a distinguishing mark of Western law. There are numerous examples in our present culture of the primacy of intention over result.

During the Enlightenment a supplementary principle was added as the basis of new legislation in Western culture: "equality of all before the law." It was a wonderful intention that became an aim of nineteenth- and twentieth-century legislation, now and again formulated in the law itself and in constitutions. But it is an intention highly at odds with the reality or the result. Great parts of our populations never get near the law, let alone before it, being subjects of prejudice by others more powerful. Lawyers' fees have usually been too high for common people, the threshold to lawyers' offices too high, and the language of lawyers incomprehensible, their reasoning obscure.

The American expression "See your lawyer" is an example of middle-class hypocrisy, as most citizens are unable ever to get near a lawyer, regardless of their legal problems. Only in very recent times have we witnessed the offering of legal aid by so-called social lawyers, and it is now questionable whether such aid will outlive the twentieth century. While equality may be intended in our system, the actual result does not seem to matter. The legal system is like a friend who invites us to come and stay but panics when reminded of the promise.

There are many instances, especially in criminal law, in which the intention to provide equality has had contrary results. Strategies to achieve the intended result have been rare. Any visit to even the least horrible of prisons in the Western world will reveal how both minorities and the underprivileged are by far overrepresented in relation to their rate in the population. Are these people more criminal than their more privileged fellow citizens? In light of the malfeasances in high office of the past few decades, who would dare to say so these days? Are the administrators of criminal justice biased? We are not allowed even to think the unthinkable. But we do get the impression that we have spent more energy in constructing a strategy for the prevention of equality before the law than for its implementation. Criminologists long ago pointed to such inequalities, but little has changed. Our system of criminal law is still based on the enduring primacy of intention.

Another example. With much care, sometimes by hook or by crook, administrators of criminal justice since the beginning of last century have developed a seemingly fair tariff based on this rule: we should proportion the punishment to the crime, be it in fines, imprisonment, or whatever. But until recently few of them took into account the eventual social result of imprisonment: stigma for life. Again, the intention is merely concerned with a "fair" imputation of imprisonment due to the particular crime, but the social reality is entirely different. In a very real sense, every prison sentence is a life term, especially in a bureaucratized society such as ours, where no person can conceal the degraded identity he or she has received from the administrators of criminal justice. The eventual social and mental consequences of incarceration are so blatantly disastrous as to make it doubtful whether good intention ever played a part. The recent novelty of advertising in the media the return to society of a former convict is the most shameless example of intended stigmatization for life.

Criminologists have pointed to this outrageous absence of justice over the past three decades, and quite a few administrators of criminal justice have seen the problem. Unfortunately, even with the best of intentions they cannot do much more than merely reduce the punitive tariffs, as they must operate within a preposterous legal system, that is, our present punitive repression. It may be *a* law or *the* law, but it is *no* law in the sense of justice. The introduction of alternative kinds of punishment will not change the scene. A punitive system, which always implies moralism, will never fail to generate the aftereffect of shame and social expulsion. The scene will remain the same: results do not balance intentions—unless the intentions are indeed hypocritical. Something similar happened with the introduction of the medical model. As therapists were doing their work within the punitive model with all its moralism, a convicted criminal from then on received two stigmas: that of delinquency and that of madness.

The conventional model of justice, then, opens little prospect of finding a fair model of crime control. Fairness simply does not fit in.

### Anachronism and the Spirit of Roman Law

For several reasons it is recommendable now to discuss Roman law. Of course, since our present model of justice originates not only from ancient philosophy but also from ancient law, this would supply sufficient reason for such attention. But there is more: the study of Roman law can make us aware of how a highly developed legal system could apparently do without an elaborate system of punitive crime control. In the Roman system, punishment was the exception and compensation the rule. Too many modern scholars have lacked the imagination to realize that crime control in ancient times might have been fundamentally different from our own method.

Here we come across an important problem of historical interpretation: anachronism. Anachronism is the tendency to make a false reconstruction of history by attributing our own modes of thought, customs, and social structures to a period of history to which they could not have belonged. Anachronistic thinking has polluted many historical surveys and analyses. Many people, even trained scholars, suffer from this hermeneutic failing. Nonetheless, modern general historians are well aware of it.[7]

The fallacies of anachronism play a regrettable role in the historiography of crime control. Professional historians, well aware of the danger of anachronism, have until recently ignored the history of criminal policy and left the study of it to jurists, who were often insufficiently trained in historiography.

One of the main anachronistic fallacies is the persistent belief that in historical development only the more suitable social structures survive. Although punitive criminal law is a rather late development in Western history and, in its present form, is a construction of recent modern times, many learned scholars in this field believe in a shaky dogma and assume that our present punitive structure of crime control depends on some kind of eternal and natural law, having always existed, though in a cruder form, and having survived because it turned out to be more suitable.

Since the punitive model is today the hard and solid backbone of
our crime-control system, untrained Western scholars have great
difficulty imagining that it might have been different in more ancient times or in other parts of the world. This leads to bizarre
consequences. For if they find in more ancient times a different
system of societal reaction to criminality, they tend to ignore it
and seek passionately for vestiges of a punitive model in history.
And many scholars, if they are willing to admit that an ancient
crime-control system was better and less punitive than the present
one, add at once the stereotyped argument that times were different then. This argument allows them to reject that system as an
exemplary model. It is a kind of reinforced anachronism.

By using the history of crime control as an example, we can
see how, even to a trained scholar, it remains difficult to assess
people's views on the organization of criminal policy in ancient
times. The mere use of the terms *criminal law* and *crime control*
in reference to ancient law and legislation is already an anachronism. After using the modern word *crime* in a historical study of
ancient law, we then apply it to a culture which, like all ancient
cultures, had no official public prosecutors and no special criminal
trials, a culture in which criminal policy was not even a part of
public law.

The Romans did not have a word for "criminal law" or for
"penal law" (*droit pénal*). Their word *crimen* still betrayed its
Greek origin. It did not mean "crime" but "charge," the private
complaint brought in by one citizen against another. The Romans
hardly knew of the idea of public complaints, except in political
cases. The semantic change that the word *crime* has undergone
since Roman times is remarkable. Reflecting on it helps us track
the dramatic change also undergone by the Western system of
crime control in modern times.

A similar semantic change can be found in the history of the
term *penal law*. The Latin word *poena* (from which both *pain* and
*punishment* derive) also betrays its Greek origin, *poinē*. Its meaning referred not to punishment but to the compensation value to
be paid in order to resolve a criminal conflict. But even if we
translate *poena* as "punishment," it still means the duty of compensation imposed on an offender; its meaning of infliction of

vengeful pain is secondary. The original meaning of the Latin verb *punire* is "see to it that the duty of *poena* be fulfilled," for an offender could usually buy off revengeful punishment by settling the compensation. To translate *punire* as "to punish" again is sheer anachronism. The best way to avoid anachronism is to be aware of the history of words.

To analyze the problem further we need to take a closer look at the peculiar characteristics of Roman law. The body of Roman law has always been civil law. That created its fame. Its public law attracted much less attention from later legislators. Anything which today we would define as "crime" was in Roman law first and foremost classified as belonging to civil law. When Roman lawyers had the concept of crime in their mind, they associated it with the need for compensation, indemnification, amends, satisfaction, remuneration, or acquittal. Their last association might have been to the modern notion of crime as first and foremost an act demanding punishment, in the sense of willful infliction of pain by some authority.

It does not follow that the Romans never punished, never inflicted pain. On the contrary. They punished slaves without mercy, but slaves were not subjects of law but objects and as such enjoyed almost no legal protection. Moreover, in the prosecution and persecution of political opponents, dissidents, defeated enemies, and slaves, Roman rulers were extremely cruel and barbaric. Punishments, however, were carried out under public law; criminal policy did not belong to this domain but rather to civil law.

One reason why Rome, despite its highly developed legal system, never had a coherent structure of criminal prosecution may have had to do with the remarkable fact the Romans hardly ever used their law for moralistic purposes. If they legislated against theft or murder, they thought in terms of compensation according to civil law and not in terms of condemnation of "immoral" behavior. When Christians were thrown to the lions, it was not because the Romans thought them immoral but because the Christians were denying the divinity of the emperor and thus threatening the unity of the empire or, even worse, the existing social order. Such people, Roman rulers thought, had to be exterminated, without any reference to legal proportionality. To the

Roman mind, morality and law were different fields of knowledge and practice, and the two should not be mixed together. This Roman attitude, though hardly known to Western legislators for centuries, can still be noticed among modern lawyers. A lawyer is usually not expected to be a moralist. Only criminal courts indulge in moralism.

Moreover, to the Roman legal mind the law did not serve to express moralistic emotions but rather to overcome them. Romans used law to modify the moralistic concept of guilt into the legal concept of debt—*culpa* into *debitum*. According to Roman law, a person could acquit himself of *culpa* by coming up to his *debitum*. That way of thinking is to a large extent obscure and unfamiliar to the modern legal mind.

Roman law concerning compensation was no exception in ancient law. It was only the refined and secular elaboration of a legal principle common throughout ancient law. Here too, unfortunately, a similar trap of anachronism awaits the scholar who studies any ancient legal order other than Roman law. To the Greeks, for example, the meaning of *poinē*, from which our word *punishment* derives, was not "punishment" but "indemnification." It had nothing whatsoever to do with modern punishment, in the sense of willful infliction of pain. The only reference to pain it may have had was to the process of finding how painful it would be to pay one's due to a person one had injured. But that is not punishment in our sense. Here lies the sting of anachronism.

With few exceptions we find compensation and penitence to be the normal solutions in ancient societies to crime conflicts, whereas revenge or retaliation was a deviance from the norm. To be sure, in old chronicles, legends, and epics from many parts of the world we hear the bards praising their admired heroes who take revenge against their enemies and derive great pleasure from retaliation by spreading death and destruction because of the harm they have suffered. But most of these stories are no more reliable than Homer's report of the Trojan War, and heroes, however much glorified, have always been rare. Retaliation was the exception, and even a hero was expected to accept compensation if it was offered by the offender. In many cultures we come across many devices to avoid revenge and punishment. Accepting compensation might even add to the hero's glory, because it could be considered a humiliation of the opponent. Only if no compensation was offered, if all other endeavors had failed, could retaliation take place, or even be required, to save the honor of the injured party. That was the law of many lands. It is an anachronism to believe that retaliation was the common law of ancient times.[8]

### Roman Public Law

There is another aspect of Roman law whose consequences we still endure. The Romans made a distinction between public law and civil law, the law of the rulers or of the state vis-à-vis their subjects on one hand and the law between and among common citizens on the other. The impact of this distinction on our Western legal systems has been so far-reaching as to make us unable to conceive any system of law in which it would not occur. The Roman law for common citizens was based on the assumed, pretended, and intended equality between partners. In the Roman Empire only a minority of the inhabitants enjoyed this equality (the others were foreigners or slaves), but the intention was there. Public law, however, was based on the primacy of inequality: the sovereign power of the ruler or the state over its citizens. Any dispute between state and citizen was sustained only insofar as the interest of the state allowed it. Real equality in public law was not provided for.

That might not prove disastrous so long as it concerned just civic relations between rulers and citizens, for administrative legality may provide a good way to avoid abuses. Public law according to the Roman system would, however, never logically include crime control. The Romans to the end of their culture kept the sharp differences between civil and public crimes. The former (the far greater part of crime control) were settled predominantly by repair and compensation, the latter mainly within the system of political control, a system that conveys the impression of merciless punitive control. But it is an anachronism to hold it up as a model for the general Roman crime-control system. That model came to prevail only many centuries later, in the sixteenth century, when the European states gradually began to seize the crime-control monopoly.

In sum, no justification for our present punitive system can be found in ancient history. We ourselves, as modern Westerners, must bear the full burden of guilt for developing this cruel, unjust, and ineffective system.

### Roman Punitive Law

But what type of crime control did the Romans have? Did they have some kind of punitive law, or did they not? As is often the case in scholarly discussions despite the stubborn denial by some, the answers found by scholars may betray their unadmitted politico-philosophical basic assumptions.

Let us try to find the facts. The Romans actually had different legal systems on three levels: for free Roman citizens, for free noncitizens, and for slaves. The latter had no rights whatsoever; they could be tortured and eliminated as it pleased their masters. Only toward the end of the empire, when their value increased because of scarcity, did slaves gain a measure of protection; they could no longer be punished or killed arbitrarily. It was nevertheless difficult to overrule a punishment inflicted by a master. The protection for slaves was that a punishment should not be inhumane—as if punishment could ever be humane. It has indeed been argued that modern punitive law can in some respects be traced back not to Roman civil law but to Roman slave law.

Free non-Roman citizens settled their disputes and conflicts according to their own legal systems. Such was usually the case in occupied territories.

But the most interesting system was the criminal law for Roman citizens. It was a system for the resolution of conflicts. During the republican period (before Augustus) there was a system called *quaestiones*, which can be translated as "court instructions." These quaestiones were competent in criminal cases. Later, during the first part of the empire (until about A.D. 300), the *praetor* was president of the quaestiones. These court rulings, however, can in no way be compared with our criminal trials. The Romans never had a public prosecution, either by the police or by an institution, except in political cases. So the praetor never acted by virtue of his office. Any citizen could begin a criminal prosecution and demand the help of a quaestio, but both plaintiff and defendant could stop the procedure immediately by mutual agreement.

In fact, there is no trace of what we call public criminal prosecution as we know it. It is an anachronism for any scholar today to use Roman examples for a comparison with modern European and American criminal prosecution. The Romans developed public criminal law only for political cases, and in these instances they were extremely cruel and barbaric. As they saw it, the empire and the imperial power were at stake.

The Romans never developed the religious notion that it was a god who wanted public criminal prosecution. Sometimes the Roman gods took their personal revenge, but that was something else altogether. And while it is true that toward the end of the empire (the so-called *domitiat*) and in the Byzantine period we find a beginning development of public criminal law, that is attributable either to the decline of Roman legal culture or to the first traces of Christian doctrine.[9]

### The Origin of Modern Punitive Law

Many theories have been formulated about the origin of punitive criminal law. In the past few decades scholars have become more and more perplexed by a Western culture that developed a well-organized public system of punishment in clear distinction from other cultures.[10] It is difficult, however, to generate a plausible and satisfying theory of its origin. Here again, because the punitive system is politically based, theories of its origin betray the political views of individual scholars. In the so-called objective interpretations of the history of criminal law adopted by scholars or lay persons, we can read off their preferences for particular political ideologies.

It is beyond doubt that the ancient legal systems that preceded our modern Western system—Hebrew, Greek, Roman, and Teutonic—did not favor punitive crime control as we have it today. Some scholars assume that the old cultures would have developed our system of punitive law if they had realized the organizational and bureaucratic possibilities that we have. But that is a fallacy. The Romans, for example, were quite capable of highly developed organizational achievements. Just think of the large armies they permanently raised for the conquest of the world and the maintenance of order in their empire: arming, feeding, clothing, and militarizing hundreds of thousands of men. It would not have been much trouble to add some punitive organization of crime control to the vast administration. But the Romans did not do it. Why not? Were these empire builders perhaps too clever for that? Did they surmise that such a punitive system would provoke more crime than it prevented?

The punitive system of crime control was created by European culture at the height of the Middle Ages early in the thirteenth century and reached its full organization in the second half of the eighteenth century. Between 1200 and 1750 it gradually developed from a civil system of repair and compensation into the system of painful public repression we know today. The first "crime" in the modern sense was not murder or homicide but heresy as defined by the Holy Roman Church. The next was witchcraft. Both "crimes" have a politico-religious origin. Only in the early sixteenth century did secular rulers begin, for the first time, to develop an organized interest in the punitive repression of what today we call criminality: crimes of violence and of property. Still, for many centuries the old systems of conflict resolution, repair, and dispute settlement survived, openly or covertly, in many countries.

The punitive system, it is generally assumed, began with the Roman Catholic Inquisition, a system based in Roman slave law. We can deduce this origin from the terminology applied. In ancient Rome, *inquisitio* (Latin for "the search for evidence and guilt") could, generally speaking, be used only against slaves, not against free citizens. The Holy Roman Church, a self-appointed keeper and guardian of Roman traditions during the Middle Ages, wanted for political reasons to make the religious life and dogmatic opinions of the faithful an object of inquisitory examination. The idea that one could be an object of examination had until then been alien to free people.

The system was soon adopted by secular authorities to bolster their own power. Thus the Inquisition stood as a model for the development of a punitive system of crime control. In an inquisitorial system there is no equality between prosecution and defendant. Repressive systems begin when the accused is no longer equal to the prosecution.[11]

Crime-control systems in English-speaking countries, which originated in the Anglo-Saxon legal system, are not much different. Without adequate argumentation, legal scholars in these countries often assume that because the Inquisition was never introduced in England, their criminal procedures do not suffer the aberrations of the Continent's. The contrary is true, for with the assizes of Nottingham, given in 1178 by Henry II, the accused was no longer an equal in procedure, as he was in Anglo-Saxon law. Real equality demands a private plaintiff and not the King's Peace. Repressive prosecution began in England with the conquest by the Norman king, who wanted to keep the Anglo-Saxon population under control. It is easy to call it criminal law, but it actually was political control.

An entirely new notion in Western culture was gradually taking root, conceiving all crime no longer as a conflict between citizens but as a conflict between the state and the accused, just as religious beliefs were no longer considered a matter between God and man but between church/state and man. What heresy had become to the Roman Catholic Church, crime became to the state and its rulers. Crime was no longer viewed as a regulable conflict but as a social heresy, the state's business. Perhaps here we have found one key to the remarkable development of such a punitive system of control in Europe. It may well be connected to the formation of the modern state.[12]

There are, of course, other causes. But whatever the cause, the consequences have been disastrous. The victim, for instance, has almost disappeared from our procedures, no longer playing a role of importance and no longer able to stop a criminal procedure by settlement without the consent of the state's prosecutors. And on top of the punitive control system we have developed a system of imprisonment that has, in many nations, fallen into calamity. The system is worst in the United States where punitive authorities, backed by a punitive citizenry, have produced an incarceration rate unequaled in any other nation, unprecedented in history, and still growing. But wholesale incarceration has not brought Americans any nearer to a solution of their crime problem; quite the contrary. For a punitive system always has been and always will be counterproductive, provoking more criminality than it checks.

## The Tsedeka Model

The tsedeka model of justice is the sensitizing concept for this entire book. Summing up its details will provide a stimulus for conceiving new structures of law.

I do not intend to offer a homily on tsedeka but rather to describe a system of tsedeka law workable in our time. The concept has to be translated to our own legal system, where it has unfortunately been ignored for too long. To make tsedeka a feasible and practical means of doing justice in a modern society, it must be made perceptible in our own system of law by referring to our present legal concepts. Most of the time we can use available concepts of present law, although some of them will need to be reinterpreted and others adapted in ways different from those to which we are accustomed.

Translation still remains a precarious enterprise: the translation of tsedeka failed from the beginning. We must proceed very carefully to avoid the errors of the past. Once the concept is well in hand, the outcome may be of great value.

### *Origin*

*Tsedeka* is the Hebrew word for "justice," although in translation we may also find the term "righteousness." It might be better, however, to leave the word untranslated, for any translation may introduce a whole set of misunderstandings that would be difficult to correct later. The difficulties can be seen as far back as the first century B.C., when the Hebrew Bible was translated into Greek (the Septuagint). Later translations into Latin and other Western languages have only aggravated the problems. The philosophy of antiquity and Christian philosophy and theology based on the thought of the ancients have interpreted a concept, sprung from a different culture, by the use of categories of reasoning allowing but approximate apprehension, if there has been any understanding at all.

Although the concept has been the subject of thought and description over more than two millennia and has been, in fact, one of the central concepts of Judaism through the centuries, it has been universally ignored in Christian philosophy and legal science or dogmatics.[13] Western lawyers, trained along the lines of Roman law or Germanic common law, either have never heard of it or have ignored it. It is astonishing that a concept such as tsedeka, so distinctly descending from Biblical notions, has never penetrated into a culture that for so long has claimed to be Christian.

In a usually unrecognizable form we sometimes come across this concept in Western theology, where it has been used to interpret relations between God and man and thus was connected to the acquisition of eternal salvation. In itself there is nothing wrong with this sort of theology, but the results of such one-sided reductionism have been unfortunate. The concept of tsedeka was never intended to serve only the understanding of the relation between God and man; equally important, if not more so, is the understanding of the relation between humans, for which purpose it has been almost unknown in our culture.

The tsedeka model of justice is diametrically opposed to the Western model of justice as discussed in the preceding pages. Its most striking contrast to traditional Western justice is the implied priority given to results over intentions. In a tsedeka model the act of justice is judged by its result, just as the tree is known by its fruit. Here it is unimportant whether it be a lovely tree or a crooked one, a substantial, solidly constructed, and well-administered legal system or a flimsy one; the only concern should be whether it generates the results we expect. In this model a legislator, just like a tree planter, must consider in advance how to secure the promised result. Moreover, the result must be in accord with the intent. If the result is not in accord with the promise, it is not just a failure of administration but much worse: justice has not been done.

One may consult many sources to learn what tsedeka means, but it is sometimes difficult to gain access to them, for psychological, political, and technical reasons. One main source is the Bible, particularly that part of it which Jews call Tenach and Christians call the Old Testament. The study of this source provokes emotional resistance in many people for obvious reasons.

Nearly two thousand years' abuse of Bible texts, especially in Christian culture, has caused a distaste for the book. The reality of so many thousands of people being burned at the stake or eliminated or degraded in the name of a Christian interpretation of the Bible has not been an edifying spectacle, and the abuse has not yet come to an end. Christian fundamentalist factions in modern society are again setting out to degrade, repress, and marginalize minorities such as homosexuals, drug addicts, and "liberals," using Biblical texts as their arms. Given that sacred scriptures are still abused in such a profane way, it requires some courage to refer to Biblical texts that might offer solutions for such an important social problem as crime control.

Abuse of Biblical texts has sometimes been the consequence of erroneous translations of the Hebrew original, caused by defective knowledge of the Hebrew language or total unawareness of the vast differences between Hebrew, Greco-Roman, and modern cultures that are so deeply rooted and expressed in language. Translations have sometimes been intentionally erroneous, in fact deceitful, because translators were inclined to cater to their own cultural traditions.

Another important source for knowledge of tsedeka is Judaic literature written over the centuries: Talmud and Midrash interpretation of Torah. It takes a lifetime to reach true cognizance of this ocean of knowledge, but fortunately for us, many authors, especially in the twentieth century, have tried to throw light on the most important key concept of this literature. The German-Jewish philosopher Martin Buber has been the only scholar willing and able to create a substantially trustworthy translation of the Hebrew Bible into a modern Western language, German. For the benefit of a reliable translation and to avoid misunderstandings, he created many new words in that language.

A next source of knowledge of tsedeka, not to be ignored in our own interest, is Western theology. Christian theology has always displayed its own interpretation of reality, its own categories of thought, its own logic, in some ways efficient for our aims. The reader will come across these categories in this book. Some jurists and social scientists may appear to be a little bewildered sometimes, since it is a discourse of reasoning they are not familiar with. This theology as a source of cognizance of tsedeka creates its special problems and risks of misunderstanding. Interpreting the meaning sometimes as "justice" and sometimes as "righteousness" may in itself be justifiable, in view of the evident semantic differences between Hebrew and European languages. Unfortunately, scholars in theology only extended these concepts to the relation of God and man. God in this theology is understood as the only just and righteous one, who in his all-embracing goodness is expected to save man. Though this notion may not be wrong in itself, the main line of thought in Christianity has been so exclusively directed toward the great beyond and justice so much interpreted in eschatological perspective that the Biblical notion of tsedeka, being intended also to apply to human relations, came to be ignored.

In Jewish traditional religious thought, more world-oriented than Christian theology, tsedeka had always been regarded as referring to both types of relations. Its orientation is toward this world and only secondarily toward the hereafter. In Christian doctrine one often gets the impression that it is just the other way around.

The inclination toward the great beyond caused a peculiar doctrine to develop in Christian dogmatics. It has been most conspicuous in Lutheran literature but has also been upheld in other Christian denominations, and its origins may go much further back than Martin Luther. This is the doctrine of the two realms, or the two notions of tsedeka. According to this doctrine, there are two administrations of this world, a sort of double-entry bookkeeping. In one realm divine grace prevails, directly proceeding from God himself, and here justice—that is, tsedeka—finds its due place. The other realm is the one of sin and sword, where violence is to be repressed by counterviolence and "justice" is admissible only insofar as this second realm is not jeopardized. The Lutheran doctrine of "the two realms and the two regiments" has become one of the most hotly disputed issues in theological learning.[14]

This Lutheran doctrine, it has been assumed, substantially contributed to the rise of idolization of the state in twentieth-century Germany. Such an argument may be gratuitous, but it cannot be

denied that a doctrine of two realms may easily generate justifications for an authoritative legal system in which anything border-
ing on justice is no longer needed. With tsedeka restricted to the
divine realm, a ruler in the worldly realm can comfortably dispose
of such an awkward and troublesome concept in approaching
human relations.

It is striking how this doctrine of the two realms evokes remi-
niscences of the legal doctrine of private and public law current
among the Romans. In the first system, the one of private law,
we find all the honest, reliable, righteous, equitable, and beneficial
principles of a good legal system—principles that also could be
provided in a civil crime-control system. In practice, however, all
this can comfortably be forgotten, since in this worldly realm we
must realize rules by the sturdy hand of whip and sword.

### A Definition of Tsedeka

We have now gathered sufficient material to give a provisional
definition of *tsedeka*: not an intention but the incessant diligence
to make people experience the genuine substantiation of confirmed truth, rights, and duties, and the eventual release from
guilt, within a system of eunomic law.

This definition is provisional insofar as its components await
discussion. I will start by discussing the first parts of the definition. The meaning of the term *eunomic law* will be discussed in
detail in chapter 2.

### Genuineness and Substantiation

Although many authors have written on tsedeka, most of my
criteria derive from the writings of Martin Buber.[15] I will try to
put his German into equivalent English terms.

The first criterion of tsedeka is *substantiation*. Buber used the
term *Bewährung* for what is perhaps the most important aspect of
tsedeka. Tsedeka has always been related to action in this way:
someone or something may be called *tsedek* (the adjective) or
*tsaddik* (the noun) if he, she, or it can successfully stand the test
of and substantiate sound reliability, genuineness, and truthful-
ness. The term may be used concerning humans or material, im-

material, or social things if they are to be tested for their genuineness. The purpose is evident: both humans and things can be tested only on the quality and genuineness of their achievements—that is, on how events have turned out.

Tsedeka has been accomplished, for example, if no one has been given a stone for bread; if people have not been appeased, cajoled, or placated with empty and unreliable promises; or if people have not been deluded with false hopes never to be substantiated. This means by implication that human beings can never decide upon their own righteousness, never confirm their own authenticity. The conclusion is up to the others concerned: they will establish their judgment. As such the concept is other-oriented. Nobody will ever know about himself, even by way of the so-called inner conscience. A real tsedek person (a tsaddik) is never aware of being one, according to old rabbinic wisdom. It is others who come to the conclusion.

Let us forgo the temptation of pointing out persons or things we assume to be tsedek. It is easier to find non-tsedek persons or situations—in our political system, for instance, where politicians, during their election campaigns often delude their constituencies with election pledges they cannot possibly substantiate. Tsedeka certainly is not the most conspicuous feature of our political theater.

With equal ease we can locate legislation in which the quality of tsedeka is entirely lacking. Inevitably our punitive model of criminal law comes to mind. It is hard to find an example of legislation in which tsedeka is more lacking. No promises of the punitive model ever come true: there is no protection of society, no teaching of norms, no decrease of criminality.

One blatant example of the absence of tsedeka is our so-called antidrug legislation. Growing repression since the 1930s has only escalated the problem, and now we pay a tremendous price for the ongoing follies of our rulers. Another example, just as bad, is the death penalty, the use of which has been accompanied by an increase in violence in those nations that favor it. A death sentence does not deter, most criminologists will tell you. The contrary is true: executions provoke people into fake heroism or blood fan-

cies. It is as if God's blessing has been on those countries that
abolished the death penalty long ago; they have had less violent
crime ever since.

## Confirmation of Truth

We have two contradictory conceptions of truth at our disposal
in the logical traditions of Western culture.[16] "Objective" truth is
one of them. It is perceived to exist independent of human experience or interpretation. The concept was first formulated by the
Greeks: a thing is true or not true. In some logics, modalities of
truth have been admitted by arguing that something may be a
little bit true and a little bit untrue, but in that case we just come
across variants of the concept of objective truth. This kind of
truth became a key principle of Western science, and generations
of scholars were indoctrinated into the belief that no more than
one concept of truth can be the scientific one, described by scientific research.

Some scholars, frightened to advance any argument not based
on objective truth, hardly dare to argue at all. Some believe they
must always disclose an objective scientific truth regardless of the
consequences. The plea of conscience is not sufficient for the dis-
closure of "objective" truth, for most often such truth is not objective at all. Both so-called objective truth and the firm will to
disclose it display the political and ideological views of the scholar
in spite of arguments to the contrary. Let it be understood that
I do not oppose the concept of objective truth in itself, so long
as a scholar is also willing to entertain a different concept of truth.

The second concept of truth found in our culture is the "relational" one. This concept implies that truth is always and everywhere a social notion, part of a structure of interaction. Relational
truth is not subjective truth or relative truth. It stems from confirmation of the hard fact that truth is always someone's interpretation of reality. Truth exists between people and is a datum to
be activated. As truth exists always within a social figuration,
within a dialogue, it follows logically that objective truth should
not always have the highest priority in thought and argument.
The concept of relational truth may be better expressed by such

terms as *sincerity* and *reliability*; truth without genuineness is falsehood and malignancy.

This concept of relational truth is as much a part of scientific tradition as objective truth. Unfortunately, the adepts of objective truth discredit the adepts of relational truth as being unscientific. The latter are usually more tolerant than the former. There is little to be said against the adoption of a concept of objective truth so long as the scholar is aware of the social results of his arguments.

With regard to truth as an integral part of tsedeka, we may use our earlier argument, that it must be judged by its result. Truth is not just there; it has to be made effectual. It has to come true within the boundary of a given situation. If such a formula is ignored, truth may be destructive where there should be salvation and conservative where there should be change. The tension between the two concepts of truth is clearest in political situations. We know about economic "truth," by means of which entire sections of a population may be reduced to desperation or large nations in the Third World be impoverished. But there is also legal "truth," which may turn society into a hell. Western culture has unfortunately developed a one-sided confidence in objective truth. Again, objective truth has value only in relation to the other concept of truth. The one should not be perceived without the other.

There has always been an opposing current in our culture that permitted the concept of relational truth to flourish. Always in the history of Western thought, wherever there has been a champion of objective truth, we find a worthy opponent favoring the other concept. For every Aristotle there is a Plato or Augustine, for every Thomas Aquinas a Meister Eckhart, for every Descartes a Pascal.

The authors of the Bible, being predominantly concerned with social relations, had relational truth, not objective truth, in mind. The tension between the two concepts may turn dramatic when people are unaware of the difference between the two and assume Biblical truth to be objective. It is the mistake made by fundamentalist users of Biblical texts, who read them as if they were contemporary law or even natural history.

Just as unfortunate has been the ignorance about the two concepts of truth in the history of crime control. In civil procedures the disputing parties usually adhere to a relational concept of truth. Here it is apparent how deeply the concept of relational truth is rooted in our culture.

The idea of a search for objective truth in legal procedure dates from the development of punitive law in the later Middle Ages. This too was a derivative of the Inquisition. If a harsh punitive model of crime control is being developed in a certain society, one must be quite sure about the case of the person who is going to be exterminated by punishment and the judge needs a fixed and objective argument, not for the benefit of the criminal but for his or her own tranquillity. That is why authors of handbooks on criminal law argue, with comfort and joy, how fortunate we are in having the "fair" trial—the search for objective truth—in our criminal procedures. A strange logic: first we develop a barbaric punitive model of crime control, then we take pride in a so-called fair trial to prevent the victimization of all and sundry.

The truth in its relational aspects, however, is much more than just an answer to the question of whether the criminal has really committed the crime and under what circumstances. It is concerned with whether we are capable of ruling out the conflict generated by the crime and how we can make life worth living again for both victim and criminal. Truth is present only if such conflict can be ruled out and tsedeka can be substantiated.

### Release and Liberation

The third aspect of tsedeka may best be rendered by the word *release*, though no word in the English language reflects entirely what is meant. Release comprises the concepts of liberation, enfranchisement, and emancipation, the logical conclusion of tsedeka. If people are liberated from repression, fear, alienation, and exploitation, then justice has been done, and there is tsedeka.

Doing justice signifies that people—victims as well as criminals, plaintiffs as well as defendants—will be set free from the consequences of conflicts, or rather that the consequences can be repaired as much as possible for all those engaged in the conflict. Such release cannot be achieved by violence against criminals or by harsh punishment, for that is injustice, which does not release people from their fears but makes things worse, pushing them into incompetence. Justice by means of counterviolence breeds violence and never proceeds toward tsedeka. Relief from fear is not achieved by locking up and storing criminals in prisons; that creates a continuous feeling of uneasiness in the nation, because the conflicts are still blatantly there like sore wounds, particularly if the incarceration rate increases rapidly. When such an increase is too sharp, prisons begin to constitute a debilitating danger in society, which can only be controlled by more violent repression and destruction and consequently by an escalation of violence. Incarceration on the present huge scale is really one of the most painful lacks of truth in our society.

Neither do we improve the situation by making prison sentences shorter. The continuous return into society of ex-convicts, usually deprived of their former identities and bereft of their normal accord with society, creates feelings of uneasiness irrespective of the length of the sentence. Social anxieties are also caused by the helplessness of neighborhoods. Conflicts have been taken out of the hands of citizens, and they are reduced to incompetence in managing their own problems.

Tsedeka, in its meaning of "release," also refers to the exoneration of the criminal from guilt and culpability. If the criminal gets a chance to repair the injury he or she has caused wherever this is feasible, the way to tsedeka is opened. Release means that a prospective future is being offered to an offender, preparing the way for him to live again with other people, a possibility denied by the present punitive criminal law.

### The Rule of Law

The relation between tsedeka and *mischpatiem* (rules of law) in rabbinic tradition has long been a topic of discussion. To generate tsedeka we need rules. Humans cannot live without rules; life would be unimaginable without them. We are far from being able to live on instincts alone. It would be difficult to make new decisions again and again in our daily lives if we had to do so in a sort of vacuum. We must predict, in one way or another, the behavior of others, and we do so predominantly by the knowledge of rules. We do admit some marginal transgressions of rules, but that serves the purpose of rendering the rules visible and observable. Usually we have even made rules concerning the transgression of rules.

Tsedeka, like any other conception of justice, is realized and effectuated by means of rules. But keeping the rules is in itself not tsedeka; neither does any transgression of rule in itself mean lack of tsedeka. Rules are like water. We cannot live without them, but they do not constitute life to us. Rules are instruments to abide by, in order to find ways into tsedeka. But rules can be abused, leading us away from tsedeka. Rules turn immediately against tsedeka if they are applied for their own sake. Rules are there for people; people are not there for rules. Rules must be part of discussion, of deliberation, of dialogue. Rules are not to be enforced but to be discussed in the first place, if one ever wants to come to tsedeka. Rules should never become an instrument in the hands of the powerful; they should rather remain what they are: a means for mutual understanding in the regulation of conflicts.

## Retaliation: The Great Misunderstanding

We have already discussed the strange phenomenon of anachronism, one of the saddest incompetencies of reason. The history of the concept of retribution or retaliation provides another example, this time part of a sad fabrication.[17] For centuries a faulty belief has been abroad in our culture. It is an unfair argument that is being improperly used for the justification of our own punitive system of crime control. It runs as follows: our punitive law may be far from ideal, but we are at any rate better off than those barbarians in the Old Testament, where blood vengeance and the death penalty were plentiful.

Hundreds of times it has been stated that the Biblical concept of talion—making the retribution fit the crime—was never meant to be an affliction of suffering to offenders; neither did "an eye for an eye" have the meaning of vengeance. Still this faulty argument has been and will be repeated by jurists, journalists, and many authors on the subject, like a litany, again and again. Another argument is even more vicious. It says that whereas the Old Testament embodied this doctrine of vengeance, the New Testament embodied one of love and mercy. Because it is utterly false, this argument is one of the most malicious humiliations the Christians have inflicted upon the Jews.

Let us look at the textual facts. We are here concerned with a gross example of intentional "error" in the translation of a Biblical text. In nearly all passages in the Old Testament where English and European translations use such terms as *retribution*, *retaliation*, *Vergeltung* (German), and *vergelding* (Dutch), we find in the Hebrew text the root *sh-l-m*, well known as *shalom*, signifying "peace." Derivations of the root *sh-l-m* always denote concepts referring to bringing or generating peace. Nowhere do they refer to inflicting harm and pain. Retribution in the sense of infliction of pain is even forbidden: Don't retaliate, for mine is the peace, says the Lord.

Where did such wrong translations come from? The origin is complex, as is the case with many religious roots. In the Old Testament world, as in most other places on the globe, conflicts arising from crime were generally settled by negotiation between defendant and plaintiff, by repair and restoration. Criminality was considered to be an act demanding repair, an injury to be erased, not by doing another harm, for that would have doubled the harm, but by relief. Vengeance may be good for heroic epics but not for everyday life. That applies to homicide as well as to lesser infractions. Punishment would arise only if the normal solution to conflicts had failed in one way or another. To assume the existence among the Hebrews of any punitive organization or any predominant punitive ideology as we know it in our own culture today is an intolerable anachronism.

Many cultures knew the institution of blood vengeance, but it was rarely practiced for fear of escalating the conflict. The practice has been recorded precisely because it was so exceptional. The "normal" is rarely recorded. Blood vengeance served the purpose of enforcement in cases where the defendant refused to negotiate, compensate, or repair.

In a system where negotiation prevails, just one type of punishment is usually practiced: banishment. And even that is not intentional infliction of harm. Those criminals who continued to refuse to negotiate after several exhortations or invitations could

be banished, for they placed themselves outside the social order.
It was not the original crime that brought punishment but the
refusal to negotiate.

Here lies the difference with our modern punitive system. In
our view, offenders have placed themselves outside the social order
just by committing a crime, and so we throw them out of society
(after a "fair" trial, of course). Once a crime has been committed
there is no forgiveness, and no activity of the offenders can bring
them back into the community, not even passive submission to
the harm we inflict on them.

Of course, refusing offenders in ancient times were often in a
sad position. In the ancient Germanic tribes they became werewolves, human beings gone wild, living in forest or desert, looking like wolves and stealing chickens from farmers just as wolves
do. But even werewolves could always return by their own initiative if they achieved their due. So, however one looks at it, the
ancient systems of crime control were far more merciful and civilized than our present system.

Still, what about the famous talion, the well-known maxim "an
eye for an eye and a tooth for a tooth"? Buber translates it, correctly, as "an eye for the compensation of an eye and a tooth for
the compensation of a tooth." This translation matches the legal
situation of the period, when no formal punitive organization existed. Do not avenge, says the scripture again and again. It does
not suggest either glossing over all criminal matters or covering
them with the cloak of charity. Perpetrators must answer for the
injury they have caused. The talion is a rough-and-ready rule for
the benefit of those negotiating reparations for injuries and damages caused by crime and delinquency. It forbids the use of counterviolence or revenge, except in the case of a perpetrator's
unwillingness to make amends. Under no circumstances does it
command any avenger or any authority to induce suffering. It
means proportionality and nothing but that.

In the ethical and juridical imagination of the authors of the
Bible, ancient popular wisdom played an important role. Proverbs
26:27 puts it this way: "Who so diggeth a pit shall fall therein and
he that rolleth a stone, it will return upon him"; Genesis 9:6
states that "who so sheddeth man's blood, by man shall his blood

be shed." In view of the cultural setting and the absence of a punitive organization, such a maxim could have no meaning other than popular wisdom: anyone who sheds his neighbor's blood should not be amazed to find people turning violent against him. Anyone in our time concluding from such a text that modern punitive authority must pronounce death sentences commits an intolerable religious anachronism, the most risky of all because of the mythical and numinous impact of ancient scriptural texts on people's minds.

A difficult factor in the origin of erroneous translations of the Biblical text concerning retribution is one of a semantic nature. In a period when crimes were considered to be injuries for which the perpetrators had to pay their due and negotiations on such pay were the usual sanctions, people needed a standard of proportionality. The Latin word for "retribution" meant the assignment or imposition of duties of war and taxation on various tribes of a city; every tribe had to contribute as taxes were distributed and repair had to be retributed. It did not mean infliction of harm but assignment of duty. Since the usual sanction on crime was the duty to repair, the legal system did not call for malevolent punishment. The later meaning of *retribution* as infliction of harm or suffering on the perpetrator came much later, after medieval times.

Things got worse when, as an outcome of the Enlightenment, the punitive model got its final shape, from which we still suffer today. The influence of the Enlightenment on the punitive model was to give a rational mold to a historical misunderstanding generated by religious anachronism. In the hands of the rational legislators of the Enlightenment, the talion principle received its present form of infliction of harm on criminal citizens. This horrible way of treating the crime problem would be entirely beyond the understanding of the authors of the Bible. Neither would the Romans have understood it, except, as I have shown, in political cases.

## Punishment and Sanction

In the Bible according to Jewish tradition there is strong evidence that punishment is ethically and morally almost impossible.

Maimonides, in his Mishne Torah and referring to the Talmud, says that if ever you punish someone, he becomes your brother—a rule that cannot easily be implemented by modern courts.[18] It is an excellent and subtle, though at the same time highly ironic and fastidious, adage whose tenor is far-reaching. The consequences of any punishment, it says, are enormous, to both the inflictor and the receiver of the punishment. Those who believe themselves empowered or entitled to inflict punishment must face the responsibility for what they do. Why should liability extend only to the convict and not to the inflictor of punishment?

The requisite of brotherly responsibility is so far-reaching that it is doubtful whether anyone could ever comply with it, certainly not our modern courts and judges, who hardly ever meet their convicts again after the verdict, except in cases of recidivism. This requisite follows entirely the general line of Talmudic thought. The Talmud, for example, never abolished the death penalty, because at first sight it seemed to be a command of scripture. But as the death penalty is so strikingly at odds with the general command of love on which the entire Torah is based, Jewish leaders made the rules of evidence so complex on this matter that it became virtually impossible to pronounce a death sentence. Any Sanhedrin in the early Middle Ages was considered outrageously harsh if it passed more than one death sentence in seventy years.

### The Semantic Fallacy

The etymological origin of the word *punishment* does not point to the meaning of infliction of harm, suffering, grief, sorrow, or injury as we understand it today. As noted earlier, the word stems from the Greek *poinē*, from which other modern terms such as *punitive*, *penitence*, etc. also originate. *Poinē* means any act of expiation or atonement which any person takes upon himself or herself to settle a dispute, be it consequent to tort or to crime. The nearest English equivalent to *poinē* is perhaps *penitence*, or even *payment*. (The English verb *pay* stems from Latin *pagare*, which has a comparable meaning of "appease" or "to settle.") It is true that in the course of legal development in antiquity a magistrate could impose a penitence, and then it was called punishment.

However, this usually happened only when the disputing parties wanted it.

The original meaning of the Latin word *punitio* was that which we understand today by *sanction*: ratification of a rule. However, the punitive model in our culture has not only distorted our legal system but has also contaminated our language. As it changed the meaning of *poinē*, it also changed the meaning of *sanction*. The Latin word means "hallowing" the order of rules, the sanctification or ratification of sets of rules that enable us to live in a society, to satisfy our needs as social beings. A sanction is a clause to a rule or a law helping us to find a regulation when conflicts arise respecting these rules. Step by step, however, as dispute-settling structures were more and more repressed by authoritarian states, *sanction* received the modern meaning of "punishment" or "penalty."

When words such as *punitio* and *sanction* lose their old meanings, we must coin new words or struggle to win back their original meanings. In this book I will try to give the term *sanction* its original meaning. Rules that help realize and effectuate tsedeka are sacred rules that need a sanction. They need ratification not by suffering but by tsedeka. That is sanction. As for *punishment*, it will be a hard job to give that term its ancient meaning.

### Suffering and Purification

Among the many traditions of our culture we find a primeval and time-honored concept. Human beings, we think, being obliged to suffer so many grievances in their lives, may take advantage of their suffering for the purification of their souls. Many of us believe that grief can be greatly beneficial for the confirmation of personality and the often painful recovery of mental health, if only we are capable of accepting such pain. It is some kind of realistic explanation enabling people to overcome the sorrows of the inevitable evils of life. It is an argument used by preachers in sermons and by professional attendants at sickbeds or during terminal care.

The comforting strength of this belief is usually positive. The hypothesis of the purifying function of suffering is based on the

actual and provable ability of many people to convert the nega-
tives of sorrow and pain into something positive, evil into good.
It is a refined spiritual masochism, a sort of mental alchemy.

The hypothesis, however attractive, does not in practice work
out except in a limited number of cases. The reality is that people
having to endure avoidable suffering as a rule show the opposite
of acquiescence. Rather, they turn rebellious in an attempt to resist, and often they turn to hatred and counterviolence.

Moral entrepreneurs in some Christian and Jewish sects have
sometimes abused religious interpretations of avoidable sorrow.
Though religion may be an effective force behind the human ca-
pacity to convert evil into good, it is not valid in cases of avoidable suffering. The faithful have sometimes been misled by the
misconception that all suffering is God's intention, the actual
inflictor of the suffering just being God's accomplice in this sub-
lunary ocean of sorrow.

In the tsedeka model of justice there is little place for belief in
the all-sufficient purifying faculty of suffering, most certainly not
when it is avoidable. It is human duty to ease suffering or make
it avoidable; there is no ethical or moral justification whatsoever
for causing pain for the sake of pain as we do in our crime-control
system.

Not only in Tenach but also in the New Testament, authors
speak of resistance to suffering. "For we wrestle not against flesh
and blood, but against principalities, against powers, against the
rulers of the darkness of this world, against spiritual wickedness
in high places," says Paul in his letter to the Ephesians (6:12).
Here the apostle uses the Greek *exousiai* (authorities, rulers), the
same word he uses in his remark to the Romans with respect to
those "who do not draw the sword in vain." How fortunate that
Paul wrote down the former text, as it is an efficient argument
against those who are continuously and abusively applauding submission to sword-drawing authorities. Not submission to a pain-
inflicting system but resistance to it: that is what we need.

The presumed positive function of suffering played a role in
the development of the punitive model during and immediately
after the Enlightenment, when rulers and reformers started the
"great incarceration," as Michel Foucault calls it. The suffering un-

dergone by a prisoner in the solitude of his or her cell was believed to purify the soul and make the sufferer more fit for free society. Such was the light shed by all the well-intended rational philosophers of the new benevolent crime-control system. We still carry out the options of the Enlightenment and inflict suffering in rational payment for injuries caused by criminals. But does this intentionally inflicted suffering really purify their souls or make them fit for society? We know it doesn't.

There are three possible procedures that might have helped it work. One would be the criminal's full reacceptance into free society as a reward for the suffering he has endured. In that case he might be capable of turning evil into good because of the reward. Nevertheless, it does not work that way. The stigmatizing effect of a conviction is far too strong. From the viewpoint of social acceptance, all prison sentences are in fact life terms.

Another possibility would be the full restoration of the criminal's disturbed relation to the victim as a reward for his suffering. But that does not happen either. His suffering prevents him from receiving that reward, since he is reduced to passive submission to the inflicted punishment and will never be able to prove he has really accepted his penitence with a good intention.

A third possibility is that a criminal's suffering would serve to prevent crime. But we know for certain that it does not; the violent reaction to criminality by the authorities makes things worse. The punitive response to crime is rather a macrosocial lesson in violence, and all violence breeds violence; punitive violence is no exception.

The suffering inflicted on criminals in the punitive model is not only avoidable; it *ought* to be avoided for the benefit of all, including victims and offenders. Avoidable suffering does not purify the criminal's soul; it achieves the opposite effect. The convict knows that his suffering serves no positive purpose, and so he rebels against it. And he is right. Who wouldn't? It is the main cause of recidivism.

Because suffering inflicted upon an offender will not bear positive fruit, it is not tsedeka. The infliction of suffering does not mean that "justice is being done"; it means that justice is being obstructed. Suffering would fit into the tsedeka model only if it enabled the convict somehow to improve the state of his own soul and that of the victim. As long as it doesn't, justice has not been done.

## Human Rights and Human Duties

Before directing our attention to offenders and plaintiffs, the nonofficial subjects of law within the crime-control system, we must consider the intriguing question of how human rights and duties fit into a model of tsedeka justice. In the history of morals some kind of balance has always existed between the two notions of human rights and human duties. True, in early Christian ethics, duties (e.g., the seven works of charity) were exceedingly emphasized. The faithful were not incited to claim their rights in order to achieve eternal salvation but were told that they had the duty to strive after it within the limits of orthodoxy. In thought and discussion duty received more emphasis than right.

Today, when rights are so much emphasized, we have gone to the other extreme. What happened to our duties? The emphasis on human rights, or rather the shift in the balance of duties and rights to rights alone, occurred during the Enlightenment. One can infer the shift by comparing the Dutch revolution against Spanish rule in the sixteenth century to the American revolution against British rule in the eighteenth century.

When the insurrection of the Dutch against the king of Spain succeeded, the newly independent Dutch government, in 1581, issued an act of abolition, with the intention to justify the insurrection and the deposition of the king. They did so by referring not to rights but to duties, arguing that a prince has the divine duty to care for his subjects and the subjects have the duty to obey their prince. But as soon as the prince neglects *his* duties, the subjects can suspend *their* duties. In a way, they even have the duty to rebel in obedience to God's law and to abolish the prince's rule, for the law of God exceeds the laws of the king. The king is there for his subjects and not the subjects for the king.

The Americans, in 1776, followed an entirely different course of reasoning. Children of the Enlightenment, they justified their acts on the basis of human rights: we have inalienable human rights; the king violated them, so we have the right to throw him out.

This shift from duties to rights may have been caused by sweeping political circumstances. The repressions applied by absolute monarchies in the seventeenth and eighteenth centuries probably resulted in the triumph of the idea of rights. A shift back the other way occurred in the nineteenth century, when people became worried about abuse of rights by the wealthy at the expense of the poor. It resulted in the formation of socialist ideas, in which duties, especially the duty to contribute to a socialist society, received more emphasis. At present we can observe some shrinking from the idea of duty, perhaps because of the Soviet experience with communism. The Soviet Union overemphasized duties at the expense of human rights.

Such shifts may have been caused by a serious imperfection in declarations of human rights, which contain a nasty virus that contaminates the entire idea. They are also partly due to general disregard for duties. Such disregard can be inferred from clauses concerning criminal law and criminal trials in all declarations of human rights.

Human rights are innate and inalienable. That is their very essence. How is it, then, that just by the opening of a criminal prosecution they can be suspended? Persons accused of crimes when being held in preventive custody and later during incarceration, are stripped of their rights and must live at the pleasure of their punishers.

This suspension of human liberties is the virus to which I just alluded. Who can enjoy human rights when incarcerated in a jail awaiting trial without any possibility of finding a solution for the conflict that got one there? Regarding the punitive system, declarations of human rights are one of the greatest hypocrisies of Western civilization. For if human rights, as all these declarations pretend, are innate and inalienable, they cannot be suspended. A human right is not a license that can just be withdrawn. Even the worst violent criminals should remain in full possession of these rights.

The repressive system, in having declared war against crime, keeps the criminalized part of the nation in a permanent state of

siege, with the definition of crime lying in the hands of government prosecutors. Governments are able to make comfortable use
of this annoying virus in declarations of human rights. Nobody
can interfere as long as the treatment of a prisoner is according
to the law of the land. Of course, the claim for due process can
see to the observance of the law; but still the accused have only
one right left.

Before the Enlightenment, the punitive system, though small,
was often very cruel; criminal trials lacked proper and just procedural legislation. So it became one of the main issues of the Enlightenment to arrive at good legislation and enforceable rules of
due process. That is fine. But because the idea of duty was neglected, the authors of the laws and declarations also lost remem-
brance of the idea of redress and penitence. When they conceived
of the declarations of human rights they were well aware that coping with criminal activities remained a problem. If they had remembered duty, they would have conceived the "right" of the
accused for a fair trial and simultaneously the "duty" of every
criminal to repair the harm caused. But instead they accepted a
suspension of rights by criminal law and in doing so admitted the
nasty virus in the conception of human rights.

Some might argue that the concept of duty is simply the mirror of the concept of right. In this view, duty is by consequence
included in declarations of rights: everyone has the duty to acknowledge the rights of the other. Unfortunately, it is not that
simple. For we have more duties than the acknowledgment of
rights. And what are these duties? Have we possibly lost the balance between right and duty at the cost of the latter? It is strange
that we have a universal declaration of human rights but no universal declaration of human duties.

As long as we do not have a well-conceived notion of human
duties, any improvement of the crime-control system is bound to
fail. We need the observance of human rights in the repressive
system and the observance of human duties in the new system of
control to be discussed later in this book. It is therefore worth
consideration that the international institutions for the defense of
human rights call into being an international commission to draft
a Universal Declaration of Human Duties.

## Guilt and Culpability

Terms for describing the intricate phenomenon of guilt and culpability are as complex and obscure as the phenomenon itself. The English word *guilt* is of unknown etymology, though perhaps related to the Teutonic term *schuld*, which is in use in all other Germanic languages. Its lexical definition is "the fact or state of having committed a legal offense or a moral wrong, implied or specified." But it has a wide range of emotional associations, such as reproach and blame, bad conscience, encumbrance, remorse, moral burden, worry, responsibility, the need for redress and accountability, and in a guilt culture, usually the need for penitence.

Nonetheless, in procedural usage within our repressive crime-control system, these associations have no specific legal value. Instead of using an offender's natural guilt feelings for the resolution of a conflict, these emotions are left untouched. As a consequence they can become very destructive, both to the offender and to the victim, who has no chance in the present system to mirror the offender's guilt.

The complex guilt phenomenon thus is reduced to being a tool for the imposition of punishment, with gravity of guilt determining the severity of the pain inflicted. It could be used for far better purposes.[19]

### Reproach

The notion of guilt implies a need for reproach in the sense of moral disapproval. One of the central notions of our moral system, guilt often leads to rage and hatred on the part of the injured party. If an offender becomes aware of what he or she has done, it may lead to self-reproach, regret, and remorse—and often to despair when the offender realizes that there is no chance to redress the harm done. Here we find one of the profound reasons for the existence of religions, by which people hope to find pardon and mercy and a way out of their despair.

Guilt can be a positive mechanism. It may lead an offender to realize the errors of the past and to desire to make amends. Frustrating this desire may cause serious disorders, and heaping re-

proach upon the offender without opening the possibility of re-
pairing the harm only compounds the disorders. Ignorance of
such a drama of conscience represents barbaric cruelty, a cruelty
experienced daily in our courtrooms. Thwarting guilt feelings
does as much damage as the deed itself, and perhaps more.

Our punitive system does not differentiate between penitence
and punishment. The former is an act, a gesture, the amends a
penitent pledges in order to get out of a desperate situation of
guilt. Punishment is a suffering inflicted upon an offender, demanding enforced submission without any awareness of whether
the culprit is mentally accepting it or not. Penitence might eventually lead to some kind of clarification and brighten the relationship between the offender and the victimized environment. But
punishment does not and never will clear up situations; such a
result is not even intended by the inflictors of punishment.

Guilt feelings after an offense are normal; they arise as the first
opening to a solution. In fact, they are the only way out of a
hopeless situation. The absence of real penitence in our present
system thus is the sting of all the difficulties. The notion of penitence, though often ridiculed and receiving no legal attention, is
in fact a divine gift.

## Guilt and Duty

The Romans, as noted earlier, made a sharp distinction between *culpa* (guilt) and *debitum* (due and duty). Both *due* and
*duty* derive from the Latin word *debitum*. If in Roman law a guilty
person accepted his duty and somehow achieved what was due,
the case could be settled. Guilt was hardly used for moral interpretation. We accept this Roman system still in our civil system
of law. Only in punitive law have we lost this idea.

The concept of moral guilt in our punitive legal system would
be less dramatic if we had stood by the original Judeo-Christian
tradition in our culture. In this tradition guilty persons have the
right to confess their sins before God and humanity and receive
acquittal or a pardon. According to the teachings of the Holy
Roman Church, the faithful will receive divine pardon and salvation through confession of guilt and performance of "good

works." In other words, the church teachings demanded some kind of performance for the acquittal of guilt. By the sixteenth century this teaching had deteriorated, having been abused by the trade in indulgences.

Martin Luther opposed that teaching with his doctrine of *sola fide*, that is, salvation by faith alone. He wanted to stress the omnipotence of God, who does not want to be blackmailed by the good works of the "faithful." Calvinist theology in the same period went one step forward on one hand and one step backward on the other. It preached God's omnipotence in predestination, but at the same time demanded that works of gratitude be accomplished by the faithful.

That may have been a reasonable theological teaching with regard to eternal salvation, but it has been disastrous in its influence on criminal law. Translated into criminal law terms it means that the suspect will be punished and be left at the incomprehensible and mysterious mercy of the criminal court, but nevertheless must accomplish works of gratitude, that is, forced labor without salvation. For the punitive organization we have constructed since then behaves like a god in heaven. Whatever offenders may offer as good works, whether they be remorseful, repentant, or willing to do their utmost to repair the harm caused, that can never contribute to their social salvation. On the contrary; once found guilty, they are lost and in a shameful way, left entirely to the tender mercies of prosecutors and judges. What these authorities have to offer is not acquittal but stigmatization for life.

It is difficult, of course, to point to any particular ideology that might have influenced an entire system of crime control. It is even questionable whether ideologies have ever been so powerful as to overturn entire cultural systems. But is it only coincidental that punitive criminal law began its calamitous course during a time of Inquisition, *sola fide*, and works of gratitude?

## Reversion and Related Concepts

Reversion, conversion, repentance, forgiveness, atonement, reconciliation, penitence: all these concepts are entirely ignored in the punitive model of criminal law.[20] An appropriate terminology for them is entirely absent, and the administrators of punitive justice would be at a loss if they had to apply them in their pain-inflicting activities. Now and again, of course, some prosecutor or magistrate, being of kind disposition and noble character, may try to find room for the realization of these concepts. Sometimes juries even consider repentance to be an extenuating circumstance. But neither reversion nor repentance has any sensible function in criminal procedure except that of extenuation, and that would not open the road to a solution. Any judge or magistrate who tries to refer to them runs the risk of being thought "soft" on criminals. But here looms the mistake, for these concepts as I propose them are by no means soft, naive, or sentimental. They are hard, real, and tangible.

There is another hazard. Kind people in the field of criminal law, intending to do good, have advocated reform by introducing forgiveness instead of punishment, atonement instead of blame, without realizing that these acts are simply out of the question in a punitive model. It is not lack of good will that causes administrators of punitive justice to be unacquainted with such concepts. It is simply the reality that the punitive system does not allow for them.

Consequently, to arrive at some kind of realization we should not just preach forgiveness and mercy without any result but try to translate these concepts, hard as they are, into applicable legal measures. That is the problem, and it can be solved. These concepts are not soft or sentimental but relevant, and they can be made appropriate for legal use. (See chapter 4.)

## Reversion

A concept from rabbinic tradition may help us discourse on such delicate notions as reversion, conversion, repentance, and atonement. I refer to the salient notion of *teshuwa*. Its basic meaning is "turn around." It stems from the interpretation of life's course as being "underway." Life is seen as a voyage toward an eventual destination, the particular aim of a particular person.

Fifty years ago the image of "man underway" was in favor among existential phenomenologists who were trying to make their philosophy somewhat clearer by reference to *homo viator*, "man as traveler." They argued that human beings, through education and primary reference groups, receive all sorts of signals marking life's course. There is a particular course for a particular person. Continuing the symbolism, it can happen that a person goes astray, losing the meaning of the signals and gradually getting lost. When awareness grows, a person may realize the necessity of turning back to find again the last "good" signal, trying from there to find the right way again. Dante used the image in the first stanza of his *Divine Comedy*, lamenting that "midway in the course of my life, I went astray; nor could I find my right path anymore." He was lucky enough to run into Virgil, who was willing to be his guide in awkward circumstances.

Turning around, reconnecting to the right signal, can be a laborious process. One might get the impression one has lived for nothing, at the same time realizing that any further progress on the same way would just mean loss of energy. The choice of the wrong road may have been caused by delusion, absence or obscurity of marks and signals, or erroneous interpretations. But whatever the cause, there is only one solution: turning around as soon as possible. Delay would make things worse. Such a decisive situation is called teshuwa.

This Hebrew concept has been translated as *conversion*, a term that now has predominantly negative religious connotations; a convert is usually thought of as self-exalted, fanatic, intolerant, and intolerable. But teshuwa does not mean a life's change toward some kind of holiness. There is nothing sacred about it; it is simply a turning from a wrong path. It is an irresistible yearning to restore good relations with fellow humans, to define once more the duties of one's life.

How does a person find out that he or she is going astray? People in one's environment may indicate their discontent, sometimes by verbal means, sometimes by physical aggression. Usually the indication is quite clear, most certainly when actions interpretable as crime and delinquency are involved. Others' discontent may be very annoying, but it is difficult to admit to oneself an error of life. Often the object of the discontent will try to justify his or her behavior. Usually we are more inclined to accept criticism from a friend or relative than from a stranger.

Acceptance of criticism, however, is subject to conditions. The most important conditions are that the critics have no personal interest in making their reprimand and do not criticize from a position of power. If these conditions are not met, the censured person probably will reject the reprimand.

There is one exception to the general rule that a critic should not have a personal interest. The person who suffers damage from any crime has a right and a duty to criticize the perpetrator, because his or her interest is genuine and valid. The criticism, however, must be accompanied by an invitation to settle the dispute, for if the motive is sheer self-interest the critic may need teshuwa as much as the opponent.

The official administration of punitive justice is no exception to the above conditions. A call for teshuwa should not be pronounced from a position of power and enforcement. Teshuwa is seriously obstructed if called for by means of punishment, retaliation, incarceration, stigmatization, and all the instruments of torture. Coercion supplies the defendant with justification for refusal and constitutes a provocation to continue an erroneous way.

Dostoyevski in *Crime and Punishment*, subtly described the road toward teshuwa. In this case it was the public prosecutor who attended to the process of teshuwa, but this prosecutor did not keep the offender in preventive detention and apparently did not abuse the power of his position. He knew that if he had applied the coercion of preventive detention, it would have obstructed the teshuwa of the offender.

In the nonfictional world of our own punitive system, all the role players—judges and prosecutors, police and criminal investigators—pretend to defend society, an often criminal society in which immoral but official practices are tolerated. This situation supplies another reason for an offender to refuse teshuwa, since he is dealing not with his victims and plaintiffs but with an all-powerful punitive organization that bears pain infliction in its armory.

The prosecuted person is fully aware that our punitive system trains its guns on the socially weakest members of the population, usually leaving the socially powerful in peace. In a world where even the most egregious white-collar crimes are ignored, defended, or pardoned by the ruling parties, where warlords may prepare and carry out their evil doings, often uncontrolled, teshuwa cannot flourish.

## Repentance

Repentance is, properly speaking, the sequel to teshuwa. Whoever wakes up to the fact that he or she is going the wrong way and perpetrating wrong acts against fellow beings may be moved to take a next step: an attempt to neutralize the negative consequences. Because what has been done appears difficult to undo, the perpetrator may feel helpless, and that may result in a quest for a means to reverse the negative and harmful results of the act.

This urge to repent needs to be accepted, to be taken seriously; it wants to exhibit itself and to express itself. But, though repentance has played a great role in the history of our culture and in the literature of human relations, if the word is dropped in the quarters of punitive justice the administrators tend to ridicule it. They consider it dissimulation, as it cannot be sincere under punitive threat. Such stereotypical thinking leaves no opening for the offender, who will always be faced with a wall of disbelief.

It is also of great importance that repentance, if it occurs, be made known to the victims of the crime. Expression of repentance cannot be realized except by efforts equivalent in their effect to giving satisfaction of debts. The effect of repentance is to make the offender competent to modify guilt into an obligation of debt. Unfortunately, within the system of punitive justice an offender may be ever so repentant but that will not help, unless there is beforehand a submission to punishment. Having long ago modified penitence into punishment, the punitive model lays an insolvable paradox on the offender. As long as the system of punitive justice exists, there is no place for this most natural of human acts: repentance, the royal way to improve hopeless situations.

## Reconciliation

Reconciliation is a natural result of teshuwa and repentance. Reconciliation implies the readiness of victims of crimes, the injured parties and their relatives, to acknowledge the repentance of the offenders, to accept their offers of compensation or indemnification. Such efforts repair damaged human relations. Teshuwa and repentance remain unsubstantial if not followed by reconciliation.

For various reasons, reconciliation, like repentance, is usually ridiculed within the system of punitive repression. This ridicule is a regrettable example of compartmentalization in our culture. It is left out of the system of criminal justice, whereas in religion, one of the main supporting forces in the origin of justice, reconciliation has always been a factor believed to bring people together, to make social life possible in spite of evil and calamities. Not without reason did Judaism institute Yom Kippur, the day of atonement and reconciliation, of reflection and hope, when Jews reflect on their readiness for reconciliation.

Repentance also once played an important role in the Roman Catholic and Protestant sects of Christendom. In pre-Victorian days, when the concept of sin was still connected with evil and wickedness and not just with sex, Christians did not dare to participate in Eucharist or the Lord's Supper without previous reconciliation with their brethren. In Calvinist regions of France, eighteenth-century presbyters used to visit their congregations four times a year, prior to the celebration of the Lord's Supper. They told the congregations that it was an abomination in the eyes of the Lord if anyone participated in the celebration of the Lord's Supper without previous reconciliation with those against whom they might have sinned. Thus we find that notaries were kept busy, in the weeks preceding the Lord's Supper, writing contracts of repair or indemnification consequent to theft or injury. Police were not yet involved in such matters, either because there were no police or crime control was left to other members of the community. This was most certainly the case in the Calvinist regions, where the police were agents of a Roman Catholic king bent on persecuting the Huguenots.

### Forgiveness and Mercy

Forgiveness is more than a simple statement by a victim of an evil act to the culprit such as "I don't mind any more what happened; I forgive you." It is rather a part of a long process of dispute settlement. It means renouncement by victims of their claims against the perpetrators after the culprits have repented, tried to repair the harm caused by their sinful acts, but found their guilt and liability too grievous and the consequent debts too heavy and burdensome to bear.

In such cases, for the soul of both victim and actor, forgiveness should get a chance. Forgiveness means the victim "gives away," remits, those parts of the debts which the culprit, in spite of willingness, is unable to achieve. It is a matter of give and take. In spite of this matter-of-fact character, forgiveness is not obviously consistent with human nature. It will usually mean a long struggle for the victims and their next of kin. Usually the victims need help and cannot achieve it by themselves. Bitterness and hatred may be the most abominable aftereffects of crime, and they tend to aggravate the guilt of the culprit. Failure of the victims to consider reconciliation and eventual forgiveness might cause further damage to their own psychic well-being, yet forgiveness can hardly be expected if the criminal has not come to recognize its necessity.

I have never heard of a punishment system that promotes forgiveness. The punitive model can be compared to medical science in the period when bloodletting was still considered proper treatment. Some patients survived and recovered, not because of the treatment but in spite of it. And sometimes offender and victim may find reconciliation in spite of the punitive model. But that is a miracle.

The use of the term *mercy* in our present system of punitive justice is a fine example of impudence. In applying a punitive model of crime control, we incarcerate delinquents, destroy their lives, maim their mental health, chase them out of society and our communities, turn them into haters of society, and provoke the growth of a criminal mind in their personality. What is worse, apparently we consider such a system to be a normal and unavoidable way of societal reaction. But still we seem to smell the rats in our system of crime control, for, as the aphorism runs, sometimes we temper justice with mercy. We temper violence with a kiss afterward! On one hand we have escalated an originally good system of justice into a cruel punitive model and on the other

hand, whenever we feel uneasy about it we suddenly discover
mercy and use it to correct an institution we deem unjust. Under
such circumstances mercy is mere impudence.

Mercy cannot replace justice. In a tsedeka model, justice *is*
mercy, the two being completely interwoven, the one nonexistent
without the other. Mercy is not the gentle and tender replacement
of a harsh institution; there is no need for that. In a tsedeka
model mercy is one of its aspects. It means the benevolent acknowledgment of a competence for renewal in every person, a
willingness for human interaction. Mercy means help by all the
role takers in a crime-control system, help given to victims and
offenders in overcoming their conflict and restoring human relations. That is also the restoration of right order. If such acceptance
is not present, tsedeka is out of the question. The use of the
maxim "temper justice with mercy" is therefore nonsensical by
implication. It should be replaced by "show mercy through justice." Mercy is just, and justice is merciful.

### The Final Definition of Tsedeka

Earlier I proposed a provisional definition of *tsedeka*: not an
intention, but the incessant diligence to make people experience
the genuine substantiation of confirmed truth, rights, and duties
and the eventual release from guilt, within a system of eunomic
law. Now, having gathered all the material we need, we may come
to the conclusion that the final definition does not necessarily vary
from the provisional one. The question is what the participants
in a crime-control system expect from it. Most of all they want
protection of society from criminality. But if offenders get opportunities to acquit their guilt, there will be protection, since there
will be fewer recidivists. If victims can participate in negotiating
conflict resolutions, there will be protection; if victims and offenders are reminded of their rights *and* duties, criminality will
decrease. And all of society will finally experience the meaning of
genuineness in crime control.

# 2

# TWO CONCEPTS OF LAW
## Anomic and Eunomic

As WE HAVE seen, the tsedeka model of justice lends itself quite well to basic formulas regarding crime control. From now on we will turn theory formation toward social and legal science as well. The question arises how we can translate the tsedeka model into feasible rules of law in modern times. We do it by using two concepts: anomie, which has been well known since the days of Durkheim, and eunomie, its opposite.

To understand our present system of law it is again expedient to make it stand out against a different system, and again I have chosen a tradition originating from ancient Hebrew thought, not so much because of a predilection for theology as for two better reasons. In the first place, in theory formation any phenomenon comes to light best when measuring its merits against another, if possible its opposite. But just as important is the necessity to account for the sometimes strange, surprising, and not always retrievable ways in which Biblical thought has influenced the development of Western law, sometimes for better, sometimes for worse. We need this opposition of law systems to better understand the complex difference between *anomic* and *eunomic* law.

## Torah and Western Law[1]

Next to tsedeka, no conception has been subject to such contradictory interpretations in Western culture as the Hebrew notion of Torah on one side and the Greco-Roman notion of law on the other. Can we ever describe all the suffering caused by desperate attempts to apply Greek and Roman legal concepts and methods of interpretation to Biblical texts, as if they were laws in the Roman legal tradition? Those attempts have resulted in denouncement, damnation, and burning at the stake of many guiltless people.

Law as defined in the Greco-Roman tradition is a set of rules enacted and interpreted by authoritative persons or bodies that are binding on all persons and groups, unless there are specific exceptions. The significance of the rules lies in their binding quality, which, if necessary, may provoke sanction and enforcement.

On the basis of a law it is possible to foretell people's behavior, because one may expect them to keep to the rules. It is of no importance whether or not people have internalized the rules; they need only keep them. Binding rules can be found not only in laws, for custom and usage also generate rules people abide by to make their behavior predictable. It speaks volumes that the Greeks used their term for law, *nomos*, to indicate the absolute binding quality of rules in nature, as we still do today. The discovery and description of laws makes nature predictable. Humans and nature are comparable; they belong together.

It is of course good that people keep rules to make their behavior predictable. Law, being the basis of interactions, enables and promotes interhuman contact. It is fine, too, that contraventions of rules can be sanctioned. People ought to be confronted by the consequences of their behavior. It is their responsibility and liability.

The sting of the ancient Western concept of law, however, lies in the tail. And this tail popped up during the later Middle Ages. As Western culture in its initial period hardly knew of the punitive model, the situation was not disastrous. As long as the sanction to contravention of a rule was no more and no less than the obligation of restoring the effects of disobedience by the transgressor, the rule could be kept without much harm and suffering.

All that changed when the Roman Catholic Inquisition began to meet supposed heresies, or transgressions of religious rules, with torture and execution: the birth of the punitive model. Things got even worse when states began to monopolize such punitive models in cases of social heresy, today called crime. That changed criminals from liable persons into social heretics by enforcing them to be obedient instead of liable. As soon as rules were sanctioned by infliction of pain irrespective of other factors, such as an offender's willingness to repair, and the state claimed the monopoly of crime control, things turned sour. The result is the present punitive system.

The opposite of this Greco-Roman concept of law is the classic Hebrew concept of Torah. To come to an understanding of this concept, we appeal again to the linguistic and semantic genius of Martin Buber. When translating the word *Torah* he did not use the German word *Gesetz*, which is equivalent to the English *law*. Instead, aware of the disastrous consequences of misinterpretation and hoping to decode the Biblical concept, he revived an old German term, *Weisung*. This term means "indication, instruction, sign, mark."

Torah is a road sign, a direction indicator. It is not a rule that orders or forbids; it is rather a suggestion to contemplate the direction one must go and an instrument that helps one reflect upon the right direction. Torah is an invitation to study the right rules of life. It is not and simply cannot be a device to denounce another human being. It is meant to be a light in the darkness of insecurity. Torah has never given ready-made solutions to trouble. On the contrary, it is a bidding to enter into endless discussion to find a solution together. The expression "law and order" is an abomination in the light of Torah. Order can never be just "there"; it has to be tracked down in an endless proceeding of trial and error. Torah is an indicator that gives reason for joy; it is rejoicing in the law and a dance toward life.

An interesting example for learning the difference between the Greco-Roman and Hebrew concepts comes in the English translation of the Ten Commandments, where it reads "thou shalt not . . ." These words cannot be interpreted in the sense they would have in modern European law. The Hebrew language does have an imperative such as "do not," but that grammatical mood is not used in the commandments. It is the future tense that is used, because the idea of the authors has been to pronounce a promise: if you keep the Torah, you will by no means kill or steal any longer. Absence of crime is the reward of law abidance. The translators of the King James Version, like many other European translators in the same period, had some notion of what was meant, for they did not translate the phrase as "do not kill" but maintained the future tense "thou shalt not kill." Unfortunately, this phrase was later misunderstood as an imperative.

In the Christian tradition—the Greek translation of the Old Testament known as the Septuagint already having misunderstood the concept of Torah by an entirely wrong translation—a law is an instrument to pronounce authoritative and totalitarian judgment on someone. When this interpretation is applied to religious questions, we get persecution of heresy. In the Hebrew Biblical tradition, law being an invitation to come and talk, to enjoy a discussion on divine revelation, such short-circuiting was hardly possible. Misapprehension of the meaning of law is the reason why Christianity was the only religion in world history to invent an inquisition; Jewry hardly ever came across the notion of heresy. Whereas innumerable Christian "heretics" have been tortured, eliminated, stigmatized, humiliated, and burned alive at the stake, the Jews know of only two heretics in, of all places, Amsterdam, considered by Jewry to be *mokum*, a city of freedom. Baruch d'Espinoza was believed by some rabbis to have denied the existence of God, according to Judaism the only indisputable truth, while Uriel Da Costa doubted the ritualism of the Jewish community. Besides, Spinoza and Da Costa were excommunicated, and certainly not burned at the stake.

The consequences of applying a Torah notion of legality in a crime-control system would be enormous. The Torah notion is in the first place a democratic principle, a bidding to all those engaged in a conflict to reach a collective solution. If in Torah tradition people could not come to a solution and needed the wisdom of a judge, his pronouncement was not binding overall but another invitation to discussion. No statement is finite or decisive. That is why the Talmud is so vast, a collection of timeless statements in unending discussions. The ocean of Talmud, as it is called, does not dispose of the shores of finite decisions; its certainty is not the decision but the security of the endless possiblity of discussion.

## Anomie and Eunomie

Anomie is a social theory based on the notion of Torah. As we have seen, the legal conception according to Torah is not repressive rule but a call for discussion. Law is not, or should not be, something adverse but a liberating agency in one's life. Discussion can have a strong cohesive effect on groups and societies. If people are encouraged, law in hand, to discuss the main problems of their social life, they keep alive a sense that law is not separating but uniting them. "Binding of the law," or rather "binding by the law," then retains the original meaning of *binding* as "knitting together."

When Jews in Europe lived together in relatively small groups apart from the rest of the population, intercourse with the law was one of the main coherent factors in their culture. Such intercourse actually obliged them to stay together, for no one can get to know the law by staying alone. Of course, let us not romanticize the past. The Jews were forced into this close togetherness, and it often reduced the possibility of individual development.

The so-called emancipation of the Jews in the nineteenth century gave rise to partial impairment of Torah understanding, which had been so prevalent among the Jews through the centuries. They had to pay a high price for their emancipation, including reduced intercourse with Torah in those countries where emancipation meant adaptation to a prevailing legal system. They had to adapt to legal interpretations alien to their original culture.

Here and there, later Jewish scholars remained aware of Torah traditions and tried to translate them to the Western culture into which they themselves were integrating. Usually, however, they consciously or unconsciously omitted mentioning the origin of the notion. An example is the school of free jurisprudence (Freie Rechts Schule) in Germany in the first quarter of the twentieth century. Legal discussion, these scholars argued in a most exciting way, is a never-ending proceeding, never leading to categorical or unconditional statements. To them the basic character of legal jurisprudence is free reflection. Strangely enough, the founders of

the school, which in any case had little impact on the development
of legal theory, never mentioned Torah.

Emancipation brought to the Jews a feeling of uneasiness, of
having lost the blessing of Torah experience. The Industrial Revolution that followed brought the perplexity of alienation not only
to the Jews but to everyone. Human beings demand from the law
support in making social life feasible. Uneasiness arises when a
legal system no longer satisfies basic needs.

This failure of the legal system and the consequent uneasiness
and perplexity are what we call anomie. The first modern sociologist to apply the term was Emile Durkheim, a Jew by origin and
education (his father was a rabbi) who, though he remained interested in religion for the whole of his scholarly life, considered
himself an agnostic, always abstaining from statements about anything beyond material phenomena.

Anomie can be compared to alienation, a concept from Marx,
again a Jew of rabbinical descent. Both Durkheim and Marx thus
had a common point of departure: Torah and Torah experience.
Their perspective was of a legal system serving collective experiences, having a supportive character, which is the necessity of ex-
periencing it, keeping it alive by common activity. Marx, however,
exchanged Torah with labor—which after all is not so strange.
Labor is part of Torah and Torah is labor. Real intercourse with
Torah keeps a man busy for the rest of his life. Labor is one institution by which Torah can be made visible and tangible. But
then it has to be labor, enabling everyone to contribute in equal
measure. If labor is split up into several categories of participation,
never granting the participants any experience of the entire work
of their hands, then according to Marx, alienation results. When
the legal system, in Durkheim's view, is split up into categories,
when all participants in that system no longer can cooperate in
its realization, then there is anomie.

The term *anomie* means literally "without nomos," without law.
But we should realize at once that law in this respect is not the
Western concept, for the term's real meaning is "absence of
Torah." We find the term *anomie* in the New Testament, applied
by Paul. He uses it to describe the Romans. He did not of course
mean to say that the Romans had no laws. He knew quite well

that Roman culture was legal to perfection. What he meant, being a Jew himself, was that the Romans had no Torah. He wanted to affirm that the Roman nation was not so bad after all, in spite of the absence of Torah—as well he might, since he was awaiting trial at the Imperial Court. Following the line of argument used by Paul, one understands that Torah is not just law in any sense; it is a token, an indication, concerning the course of life.

We must admit, though, that features comparable to Torah can be found in other ancient legal systems, because they did not yet have the punitive model. The Roman system of private law, for instance, is based on discussion. Yet the Romans undermined their legal system by introducing public law, thereby opening a gateway to anomie.

In the old days, Durkheim argued, knowledge and use of rules proceeded mechanically. Society was structured in such a way as to allow people to participate in the experience of its rules. At the present time (around 1900), Durkheim continued, the function of participation in the legal system is served organically, by specified institutions (he speaks of organic law), and people can no longer enjoy personal legal experience. When this happens, feelings of insecurity and helplessness arise, discontent and rupture emerge. We are confronted with an increasing disuse of our normal abilities to cope with our conflicts; in short, we suffer from anomie and alienation. Abilities no longer used will atrophy. Anomie is a lack of rules, not of rules in general but of rules that support life. Anomic rules are no longer functional for our lives. If life-indicating rules are available, there is eunomie; if they are lacking, there is anomie.

It is remarkable how many social scientists have ignored the Torah background of Durkheim's conception. The scholar himself can be blamed for it a little, for he did not mention the origin of his theory. Perhaps he assumed it to be self-evident. Nevertheless, if in sociological literature the concept of anomie is translated as "normlessness," the author betrays his ignorance. It is not a lack of norms but a lack of the supportive qualities of norms and values.

It is evident that the rise of bureaucracy has largely contributed to people's anomie. Powerful bureaucracy and Torah experience are at variance. Bureaucracy tends to take conflict discussions and dispute settlements out of the people's hands. Looking at legal history we find that discussion of crime conflicts has also been taken away from people. Our system of "justice" is in fact nothing but a punitive bureaucracy, commissioned to prevent people from solving their own crime conflicts. Whenever communities lose the experience of rules of law, anomie will arise, and thus one can argue that the system of punitive justice has been one of the most striking examples of anomic law in our culture.

The rise of the punitive bureaucracy coincided with the rise of the Industrial Revolution. Even if the authorities of the time were not aware of it, the punitive model was introduced not for the protection of communities against criminality but to create structural conditions favorable for the development of industry.

A similar history is noticeable in today's Third World countries. Until recently, most of them had not developed a system of punitive justice and in consequence were blessed with little criminality. Crime control was effected by an assensus model. The colonizing powers had not considered it in their interest to introduce a punitive system except for political reasons to enforce colonial rule, just as the Romans had done. Since decolonization began, these countries have been trying to obtain Western investments for the sake of industrialization. The entry of capital required large investments in property. And that brought in industrial entrepreneurs who needed a punitive bureaucracy to protect their investments. Now a punitive model is being crammed down many nations' throats, and the result is anomie and criminality.

Does this mean that a punitive model is necessary to industrialization and a free-market economy? Most certainly not. Some historians, out of a kind of historical fatalism, do indeed argue that a punitive model is the natural system of crime control in the wake of state formation and the Industrial Revolution. And it is true that in the United States the exclusive punitive bureaucracy originated at the very beginning of state formation, and the Industrial Revolution soon followed. But were they indispensable concomitants?

A punitive model arises, it is sometimes argued, because the

growth and mobility of the population no longer allows community-based crime control. But many institutions, such as schools,
churches, companies, and crafts, continue to exist on a small scale.
Why then can we not have community-based, anomie-preventing
crime control? It is time to put our mind in real earnest to the
study of an alternative, nonpunitive model of crime control, no
longer obstructed by the argument of its infeasibility in large-scale
industrial societies.

I will not give in to one of the most frustrating peculiarities
of sociological theory formation. Quite often sociologists have
been marvelous in describing deficiencies in society, but their scientific disposition keeps them from suggesting cures. Durkheim
was no exception and that's a pity, because it would be great to
have his observations on eunomie. So, after these elaborations on
anomie, I turn to a discussion of its opposite, eunomie.[2]

The description of eunomie can be less difficult if we keep a
right understanding of anomie in mind. We speak of eunomie if
participants engaging in a system of rules experience the system
as supporting their lives and their social interactions. Eunomic
rules allow people to resolve their own conflicts, keeping the
awful feeling of alienation out of their lives. Eunomic rules are
Torah rules.

In the rest of this book I will try to describe a system based
on eunomic rules. Two points must be kept in mind. A eunomic
system of rules does not automatically lead to guaranteed results.
The system offers a practical feasibility. Results of tsedeka can be
assessed, but a eunomic system, as it needs realization by all participants, offers a promising working possibility—no more, but
no less, either. A eunomic system needs concern and interest. The
responsibilities are laid on the shoulders of all concerned, with a
precept for action. Above all, when setting forth the character of
eunomie in this book I am describing formulas and rules facilitating the regulation of crime conflicts without punishment, for
punishment and eunomie are like fire and water: they don't mix.

Again I repeat: it will not be a soft, guilt-denying system meant
to coddle the criminal. No, a eunomic system is useful for both
criminals and victims, or rather defendants and plaintiffs, in find-

ing collectively a way out of their often intricate problems. It will benefit not just the offenders but also the victims, their relatives, and their communities.

Another difficulty in the discussion of eunomie is the need to refer to legal systems of former days and to systems of other cultures. Everyone realizes that legal rules and formulas from long ago or from other parts of the world cannot be reintroduced without fundamental change. In the form history transfers them to us, they are often impracticable, particularly with regard to our usually large-scale, mobilized societies. We need to clear away their obscuring features and find the concept behind them in order to make them useful in our time. Such a method does not set back the clock but rather makes us aware that at a given point in history, things went wrong.

## Anomic and Eunomic Systems

In the next paragraphs we will discuss the most striking peculiarities of a punitive and repressive system of crime control as distinct from a eunomic system.

### Disruptive vs. Communicative

In the present repressive system of crime control, offenders charged with serious crimes are removed from their social surroundings, arrested, and kept apart from the human beings with whom they usually live or work: family, mate, friends, colleagues. Such offenders quite often suffer from anomie even before their arrest. They have little affinity for rules of law and often have not had the chance to learn the rules. Good law, of course, would ensure that everyone learned the rules and how to use and appreciate them. But punitive law is not made for the offender.

To make things worse, offenders get no opportunity to continue or set up contacts with those persons who have suffered from their acts and with whom they have come into serious conflict. Because they cannot contribute to a resolution of the conflict, their experience with the law will most certainly not improve their already deficient respect for its rules, let alone give them an opportunity to learn to use the rules. A eunomic system of conflict resolution might provide an excellent opportunity for offenders to learn these rules, but our present repressive system does exactly the opposite. It teaches them to hate the rules.

The victims and their friends and relatives, on the other hand, feel abandoned by a repressive system of law. Punitive laws may teach us how to repress the offenders but not what to do with the victims, who are generally left to find their own solutions.

A repressive system thus disrupts social contacts and in this way supports anomie. A eunomic system of crime control leaves social contacts intact. Offenders are not taken from their surroundings; they remain among their peers and receive the possibility—even the demand—of reaching a settlement with the victims. And while they negotiate a settlement they can learn the proper use of eunomic rules.

Not only the perpetrators but also the victims in a eunomic system are given the chance to contribute effectively to the resolution of the conflict by pleading their cause. The victim too can be surrounded by his or her own group. The eunomic system therefore is communicative. It brings people together instead of keeping them apart.

### Vertical vs. Horizontal

In the present repressive system of crime control, offenders are held against their will in a vertically stratified, punishment-inflicting institution, military-looking, uniformed, and warlike (it is, after all, a "war on crime"). It can hardly be done in any other way because the repressive system defines crime as acts directed against society as a whole and society, represented by the state bureaucracy, is obliged to take forceful action. That is the necessary consequences of the definition.

The functionaries who impose the rules in this repressive system—prosecutors, judges, jailers—are the only ones with much knowledge of the rules. Most offenders and victims remain ignorant of them, and that is how the system intends it to be. Knowledge of the rules by those being "served" by the system is unwelcome. It might burden the work of the controllers. Only accomplished recidivists get a chance to learn the rules of the system. But then it has become the clownesque role of someone who knows how to behave on the downstairs ladder of power.

In a eunomic system, on the other hand, the structure in which the rules are applied is horizontal. People acting in such a system can look at one another, learn from one another, and develop a better understanding of how to resolve their conflicts. They are no longer submitted to painful experiences in a system bent on destroying or silencing them, whether they are offenders or victims. For in a eunomic system, punishment and suffering are not imposed; only a settling of conflicts is expected.

### Inquisitorial vs. Responsive

The main justification for the existence of repressive procedures is the attempt to find the truth, that old objective of the Inquisition. The means by which the repressive system seeks its truth are overwhelming in their destructive force: the mental and physical torture of incarceration even before trial, suspension of civil rights, mental maiming and blackmail. Just under the surface of our "civilized" trial practices, physical torture always looms. Criminal trials are in themselves transgressions of the idea of human rights. Or better: in all the declarations of human rights so far, exemption has always been made of those being legally prosecuted. To justify the system or to find some tranquillity for their own souls, legislators have produced extensive sets of rules to give an outward appearance of justice, of something that might be called law.

There is nothing admirable in the longing for "truth." It does not serve justice but only the conscience of the controllers. They are not after relational truth, which might help restore human relations, but so-called objective truth, to be wrung out of suspects in such a way that they can be convicted.

The eunomic system, on the contrary, is responsive. It demands responsibility. Offenders are not expected to undergo punishment in a passive way; their active cooperation is demanded, not toward their own destruction but toward the release of their guilt. In this system, offenders are incited to respond like human beings, not in brutal interrogation sessions but in discussions and conflict settlements. Unraveling conflicts does not humiliate offenders but attempts to find satisfying solutions for all parties.

### Informative vs. Educative

According to the repressive theory, both light and heavy punishments are supposed to deter, serving to inform any future offenders and society as a whole that infliction of pain is the consequence of certain types of behavior. But this notion of deterrence rests on an incredible superficiality. One may hear people say that they were once fined for transgressing the speed limit and ever since have been more careful when driving their car, but has anyone ever remarked, "I once committed a murder, but since I have been punished I won't do it again"? Still, in spite of its shallowness, the notion has almost replaced retaliation as a justification for punishment. It appears to some people to be more civilized.

It is questionable whether this deterrent information actually reaches would-be offenders. Many people are never informed that any kind of punishment ever takes place. They have some inkling of it, perhaps, but the mass media seem to do their utmost to keep the public uninformed. It is also questionable whether such information on the repression, if received, really leads to the goal intended by the administrators of pain. If a system responds to violence by repression and punishment, the information picked up by would-be offenders might even be the opposite of what was intended. What they do in fact often learn is that a violent answer to violence is the right thing, because that is what is done by the rulers of society, who are expected to set the right example for other citizens. Here lies the real reason why the repressive system provokes more criminality than it prevents: it teaches the use of violence to whole nations. Fortunately, most people refrain from crime in spite of the bad examples.

The eunomic system, on the contrary, is educative. It inspires participants in the system to work out their conflicts and disputes. They learn norms not by pain and suffering or by the violent example of punitive controllers but by talking about norms in difficult situations. The normative learning process cannot be fostered by fear of pain, only by identification with good examples.

Norms and rules are there in the first place to make human life possible and to solve conflicts among humans, not just to deter action or to incite fear.

### Provocative vs. Invocative

Scientific investigations of the past hundred years, especially psychoanalytic investigations, give a clear indication that infliction of punishment has a provocative outcome. It does not deter crime but rather provokes potential offenders. Our society is so rife with social masochism—we are, after all, a culture of guilt and culpability—as to make people seek out punishment in the hope that they can do penitence for their crimes, real or imagined. If punishment is on special offer by a punitive organization, people will present themselves for punishment. The message of our punitive crime-control system is like a grim paraphrase of the words of Jesus: come all ye who need punishment and we will make ye suffer.

A eunomic system, on the contrary, is not provocative but invocative. It invites offenders to help resolve the conflicts they have caused themselves and others. Sooner or later they will realize that solving the conflicts is very much to their advantage, that lost or damaged human relations can be repaired. Such an invocation may give them a renewed feeling that law is made for them as well as for others. Provocative enforcement exacerbates already existing anomic feelings, whereas an invocation to discussion enhances eunomic feelings.

### Servomechanism vs. Organic

A servomechanism is a mechanical control system in which a smaller mechanism automatically keeps a larger one in motion. We find servomechanisms at work in many places, from steam engines to the most modern motorcars. A repressive crime-control system is a kind of servomechanism in a large political power system, the modern state. By the selection, definition, and prosecution of punishable offenses, a repressive system helps perpetrate existing power structures. Certain types of behavior that are punished in one particular structure may be legal in another structure. Radical criminologists have occupied themselves with such problems for the past thirty years.

A state's use of a repressive system as a servomechanism looks inevitable. State power, based in the social contract, is now accepted by the majority of most populations. Nothing wrong in that. But to crown it all we have placed the implementation of punitive criminal law entirely in the hands of the state. The state has the monopoly on violence. It would indeed be obtuse if any state power did not seize with both hands this opportunity of exercising a repressive system as a way to guarantee its own survival. One can hardly blame it for doing so. Of course, state powers have been very reluctant to exercise punitive criminal law against themselves; that might bring their own ruin. They have not only a monopoly on violence but also a monopoly on defining crime. Usually they follow the citizens' general feelings about crime definition, but certainly not always. Why should they? Such a situation, of course, results in anomie in the population except among those citizens who identify entirely and uncritically with anything the state does. The state monopoly on crime control by definition divides the population into hunters and game birds, the former believing that the legal system does not protect them and the latter certain that the legal system is always against them. Anomie is the order of the day.

The eunomic system of crime control, on the contrary, is organic; it has the wherewithal to bring people together. Once conflicts resulting from crime can be resolved by discussion within existing structures of law and custom, social and legal structures will be supported without direct reference to political servomechanisms. Of course, political issues may enter into discussion, but they cannot be so easily enforced by the powers that be.

### Frustrative vs. Therapeutic

Most people like to get rid of a conflict as soon as possible, unless in rare cases, they want to keep it alive for political reasons. But if people are cut off from the possibility of intervening into their own conflicts, as in a repressive system, the consequences are very negative—anomie again.

A crime conflict usually results in ruin. Criminals, often having been born into anomic situations and having pushed themselves into further conflict by the crimes they have committed, are pushed much further into anomie after their arrest. Repression, along with the impossibility of improving their situation by any offer of repair, makes later social assistance or probation a shot in the dark. It is a ruinous, frustrating experience for all people who want to contribute to the resolution of their conflict but are prevented from doing so.

Neither do victims have an opportunity of intervening in their own situations. They likewise are frustrated, suffering a further ordeal in addition to the misery they have already gone through because of the crime committed against them. Their conflict is stolen from them. The repressive system redoubles an already too-painful situation.

A eunomic system, on the contrary, is therapeutic, both for the accused and for their victims. If offenders are no longer subjected to repression but rather are summoned to contribute to the resolution of their conflicts, they get a chance to learn to use rules and to appreciate them. The same holds true for the victim. The wound of the crime is not healed by the destruction or repression of the perpetrator but by resolving the conflicts through discussion. The result will be balm to the soul, not salt to the wound.

### Irrational vs. Rational

The belief that the mandatory reaction to crime is infliction of suffering, exclusion, humiliation, and stigmatization is based on prejudice. The stereotyped argument is that the vast majority of people want evil to be met with evil, violence with counterviolence. People demand revenge and retribution, the story goes. But there is not the slightest evidence that this is true.

If an interviewer asked passersby whether they were in favor of the death penalty in cases of gory crimes, in many countries more than 50 percent probably would give a positive answer. But if those same persons who said they favored the death penalty were shown realistic film shots picturing executions by firing squad, decapitation, strangling, gassing, poisoning, hanging, and electrocution, including the death rattles of the executees, most of them would grow green about the gills and the number in favor would fall precipitously. What people really mean when they say they favor the death penalty is that they are scared of violence and don't want violent criminals around them. The most direct way of expressing this is "kill 'em." Calmer voices might suggest sending 'em to an uninhabited island.

A far better question to ask is whether people prefer executing criminals or getting them involved in cooperative efforts to reach a resolution of conflicts, thus cleansing society not of wayward people but of violent conflicts. The answers in favor of a eunomic system undoubtedly would be greater than the number in favor of the death penalty.

The repressive system is based entirely on an irrational belief system. Next to racial prejudice it is one of the coarsest examples of dangerous irrationalism in our culture. Like racial prejudice, it is not innate in human beings; it appears later, usually through imitation and bad education.

A eunomic system, on the contrary, is highly rational, based as it is on the rational use of existing structures of law. Eunomic law agrees with the law in general, with law that we know by nature and custom. Capacities that have always been present in human beings are used; that is why it is rational and reasonable. Dispute settlement demands the use of reason. Eunomic law is what the scholars of natural law through the ages have always adhered to: a rational law for the rational resolution of conflict.

### Enemy vs. Opponent

A repressive punitive system is like warfare. Inflictors of punishment, like generals in a war, tend to deny their adversaries the status of human beings. How often has a criminal been called the state's number one enemy? We need to believe that criminals are different from us in order to overcome our moral hesitation. Any crime we ourselves are never allowed to commit against other human beings is now permitted against "the enemy." That is how we prosecute criminals. And how often have the rulers of our society talked about their "war against crime"? Or "drugs," or "corruption," or "moral decay"?

If a eunomic system of law were given a chance to be used in the control of criminality, people should still dislike crime. It would clear the air if the people involved got a chance to express how horrifying crimes are and how bad criminals can be. But at the same time, the offender's humanity must not be doubted. An enemy can be eliminated, but an *opponent* is a partner in discussion, whose humanity can not be disputed.

We can compare the situation to the development of parliamentary democracy. In some countries, unfortunately, political opponents are either destroyed or tortured to death. These countries have anomic political systems. In such countries, not even the powerful feel at ease, because they may be overthrown tomorrow and suffer the same fate they inflicted on their opponents. In other countries, called democracies, we discuss political problems in order to reach a solution. These countries use a eunomic political system for the solution of their political conflicts, so they know quite well what a eunomic system is. It is strange indeed that these same democracies do not institute eunomic models of crime control. Rulers in eunomic democracies do not grant to offenders and their victims the eunomic rules they apply to themselves. It is one of the riddles of history that at the moment when modern Western democracies came into being, at the end of the eighteenth century, they excluded from democracy one of the most important tasks in any culture: the control of crime.

### Criminalization vs. Real Law

The power which a repressive crime-control system disposes is outrageous. It can arrest people, corporally or mentally maltreat them, incarcerate them for long periods, and in many countries put them to death. This sort of repressive action is entirely unknown in the rest of our legal system. To give this repressive system the appearance of law, a refined and complex set of rules has been worked out allegedly for the protection of suspects. Actually it concerns only rules for using violence against violence. Such rules are found nowhere else in our legal system except in the laws of war.

The repressive system has never been intended either to protect suspects or to control evil in society. Quite the contrary. As everyone knows, some sectors of society have a far greater chance of evading the punitive system than other sectors have. Our legal rules actually select certain categories of people and "criminalize" them, stamp them as criminals, but not because they are the most dangerous persons in our society. Other persons are far more dangerous, including warmongers and arms makers. It is this selective power that makes the repressive system so incredible.[3]

A eunomic system, on the contrary, is not based on exceptional rules of "war"; it is a part of the general legal system. If criminality takes place somewhere, general rules of law are applied. We must look to those rules that are used elsewhere in society for the resolution of conflict and use them also in cases of criminality. Of course, we should not live with the illusion that eunomic laws will never be abused. But in a eunomic system the chances are smaller, because a far greater variety of people participate in striving for justice and preventing abuse.

### Dysfunctional vs. Functional

A social system can be recognized by the effects it has on other systems and on human beings. Many of these effects are intentional, others accidental. As often argued in a functionalist theory, a social system would be, for the most part, the sum total of the effects it has on other systems and on the participants in the system. A system would consist of its functions. Even if we reject such an overall functionalist theory, we must admit that these effects are of great importance. A repressive system of crime control has some very intentional functions, often blatantly spelled out by representatives of the system: deterrence, retribution, prevention and control of crime, protection of society, and prevention of blood vengeance and lynching by victims and the general public.

But does the repressive system stand the test? What we see in reality is a system that has had a monopoly on crime control in Western culture for two hundred years while "criminality" has not visibly decreased. In many countries it has increased. Of course, great changes in society have also taken place, but one might have expected an efficient system to have coped with these changes. In spite of this blatant incompetence, defendants of the system continue to believe stubbornly in its functionality. The only thing they seem willing to change is the amount of repression. They favor even more punishment, more prisons, more police—more of what isn't functional. It is high time we open our eyes to this dysfunction. With any other social system we would long ago have tried another approach. But the repressive system just hobbles on and on. It is as if doctors, in spite of modern medicine, continued to practice bloodletting.

There is sound reason to see repression as dysfunctional. Not only does it fail to have its intended effects, but its results are even the opposite of those intended: repression provokes crime instead of preventing it. We can quite easily infer this result from experiences in those countries that, in spite of all warnings, rendered their crime-control systems even more severe and repressive. They got more and more criminality. Perhaps they deserve it, for they did not take to heart the lessons they could learn from dysfunctionality.

The causes of dysfunctionality are complex. A most important cause is that a repressive system uses rules alien to human nature and alien to rule making in general. The situation can be compared to the Roman Catholic Church, which, in the worst period of its history, was preaching evangelical poverty and social engagement on one hand while on the other hand giving itself over to pomp and circumstance, to the politics of power, and to the mindless repression of heresy. And so it is with the repressive system. On one hand it promises a decrease in criminality and maintenance of law and order. On the other it uses violence, applies rules not deserving the fair name of law, and sees an ever-rising crime rate. Dysfunctionality is one of the main causes of anomie.

A eunomic system, on the contrary tends to be functional. It appeals to capacities for conflict resolution that are latently present in all human beings. The people most concerned are themselves involved in reaching solutions. The chances of reaching intended aims are much greater when a rational and organic set of rules is used.

## Stigmatization vs. Liberation

In the old days, slaves and criminals were literally stigmatized, that is, branded with a hot iron somewhere on their body. Sometimes the sign served to identify the owner of a slave, sometimes to indicate a person's crime: a T for theft, an R for runaway. Sometimes the arms of a city were branded on the offender's skin in the hope that a recidivist could later be recognized.

Although corporal stigmatization was abolished early in the nineteenth century, social and mental stigmatization has continued to the present day.[4] Repressive bureaucracies recorded punishments so that the authorities would always be informed about recidivism. With our present computerized data banks, we can do that sort of thing even more effectively. Anyone who has once been condemned to incarceration will suffer a whole lifetime of stigmatization. The degradation is so strong that a convict can forget about ever returning to a normal life in society. Ex-convicts often must tell complex lies to hide their punishment. One can hardly expect this circumstance to contribute to their reintegration into society.

The effects of stigmatization have led to the great sham of the repressive system, one of the great hypocrisies in our society. For learned punitive lawyers have tried to set up a system in which the length of incarceration fits the seriousness of the crime. But they always intentionally ignore the added effect of stigmatization, which is after all a life term from a social point of view. And yet advocates of the repressive system hypocritically believe they are doing society good while every year sending hordes of punished persons back into society as ex-cons, forever unadapted and unable to make a living except by crime. At least they keep the punitive system and its lawyers and judges busy.

A eunomic system of crime control, on the contrary, has a liberating effect. Of course, offenders must bear responsibility for their crimes, and sometimes we may demand great efforts from them to repair the consequences of their acts. But because offenders get a chance to make reparations, they also get the possibility of liberating themselves from guilt. Other persons will be more inclined to accept an offender who has shown a willingness to help resolve a conflict. The garment of penitence does not disfigure the penitent. If offenders get a chance, even a small chance, to show their good will, they will not be stigmatized.

## Ritualism vs. the Piacular

According to Hegel, the great German idealist, crime is a negation of the order of law. Such negation must be met with another negation—punishment—to come up with a positive, as if it were algebra. If social reality were only so simple! Yet Hegel has given in a few words a very good insight into the punitive system. It is a system pretending to yield positive outcomes by negating the negation of order. To make us believe that the system does positive things, its controllers use rites. A punitive procedure (trial) is one of the great rituals of our culture. Just look at them, those actors in their black or purple gowns, their bands and ermine caps or berets, sometimes even wigs, sitting in majestic halls, speaking in ceremonial tongues usually incomprehensible to the commoners: their great pomp and circumstance is intended to show the majesty of the repression of evil. Together with royal or presidential parades, trials and sentencings are the top-drawer ceremonies of Western society.

Still, in spite of all these efforts there is a discordant note in our repressive system of crime control. This ritualism covers up a legal monstrosity which we call criminal justice. It constitutes what Durkheim called negative ritualism, a name he gave to institutions not about to change anything but merely wanting to show off rites. Such a ritual amounts to sacred mendacity. The system's machinery can have only negative effects on society.

A eunomic system has much less need for rites, and it is unlikely to degenerate into ritualism. We can develop a system of law that really brings a resolution of conflicts. In such a system, offenders would be given a chance to repair the harm they have done by performing piacular (expiatory) actions.

# 3

# THE ASSENSUS MODEL

THE AFTERMATH OF crime is often dramatic because our perception of it is usually connected with the problems of good and evil, right and wrong. Such a direct connection arouses emotions and makes us call for redress. This reaction is normal and human, and if in cases of violence the sequence of events is tense, that is natural. Not everyone is a stoic philosopher. In many discussions of crime control, unfortunately, the search for a definition of good and evil is left out, affecting the arguments often in negative ways. In view of the importance of the matter and its often serious effects, we must first find out whether we can agree not only on the ways in which crimes in our society are usually defined but also on the ways in which their consequences are assessed.

We know from everyday experience that defining crime can create great difficulties. What you term execution, I might call homicide; the person you call a freedom fighter, I might call a terrorist; and what you call use, I might term theft. And the definitions of crime differ not only among persons but also in relation to time and place. Yesterday's crime may not be tomorrow's crime, and a crime here may not be a crime there. Regarding the problem of crime definition, we suffer apparently from one of the most elementary human deficiencies: lack of precise knowledge concerning good and evil, the primordial predicament of humankind. The Biblical myth of what happened in the Garden of Eden was an attempt to give a religious explanation of this human incapacity. Man was created good and had, in consequence, knowledge of good but not of evil. In the Garden of Eden, humans succeeded in getting acquainted with evil, to our utter confusion ever since.

We are too good to be entirely evil and too evil to be entirely good.

We have tried, of course, to work out legal definitions to help us. But these definitions are of only limited help. For words of law must be put into practice by statements of a court, and who would agree with all the verdicts pronounced by all the courts on this globe?

If it were easy to know good and evil, the definition of crime would not be so much of a problem. If it were easy to distinguish between right and wrong human performances, we would not labor in assessing the consequences of crime. But defining and assessing good and evil are thorny matters, and whatever the system of crime control, it is our duty to find a solution. We cannot simply shut our eyes and appease our conscience by thinking that law has solved most of the problems. Ignoring the definition of crime and refraining from the assessment of consequences would be worse. Society could not endure.

Since the beginning of human civilization, people surely have tried to find the right way in the thorny fields of good and evil by more or less successful definitions of norms and values. But that only put off a solution because norms and values themselves can be defined in endless ways.

Through centuries of trial and error, people in Western society have followed three roads in coping with the problem of defining crime, and on this basis we can distinguish three models for interpreting norms and values: the *consensus model*, the *dissensus model*, and the *assensus model*. From the viewpoint of sociolegal theory these three models are ideal types, meant to sensitize our thinking. In society they rarely if ever appear in pure form. I will analyze them separately, in order to come to a better understanding of the problem of crime definition, the assessment of its consequences, and the arrangement of crime conflict and its resolution.

## The Consensus Model

The consensus model presumes that there is basic agreement among the members of a society with regard to the interpretation of norms and values.[1] Any conflict emerging from the generally accepted interpretation is considered such an unacceptable threat to an orderly society that strict rules are enacted for clearing away the conflict. This clearance is carried out by a stratified organization of administrators of justice, representing and personifying the assumed fundamental agreement.

The consensus model is in reality one of the boldest, most megalomaniac conceptions society has reached for social control. With fear of divergence and uncertainty so great, effective measures seem necessary to rule out all ambiguity once and for all. That applies to our present system of crime control. In the Age of Enlightenment, during which the bulk of our institutions of crime control originated, an excessive confidence in the abilities of legislators made people believe that courts had to do nothing but pronounce the words of the law. The law, however, does not clearly specify under what cultural circumstances human acts can be called crimes. Administrators of justice (and in some countries their helpers, the jurors) have for that reason been endowed with the monopoly of interpretation. The result is that a creature from outer space would be perplexed on our planet to see that person A kills person B and is invested with a medal of honor, whereas person C kills person D and is arrested, convicted, and executed.

The problem lies in the craft of our semantic skills and the vileness of our justificatory logic. Nobody denies that theft and violence ought to be considered unethical or immoral. Even a professional thief will admit that theft is objectionable when the thief is the victim. The most violent gangster and the most bellicose military commander will say that violence carried out against them is illicit while considering their own identical acts to be acceptable. Politics is even more frightening, because there the ends so often are thought to justify the means. The military computes death rates in "limited" nuclear wars, the administrators of justice desecrate convicted human beings by using them as "deterrents" in national anticrime crusades, and the most massive war acts are called surgical bombings. Our skill for putting violent words in sheep's clothing is overwhelming; think of ethnic cleansing.

With the wide divergence in ethical matters, the rulers of Western society have thought it necessary to appease their people. To avoid troublesome questions, crime controllers have invented the consensus model, which assumes that most of us agree on moral and ethical matters. This model implies that fear of anomie is not justified, that we don't need to panic. Once the model is generally accepted and immense moral and political power is turned over to police, courts, and prison administrators, no ethical problem exists, for these officials are presumed to personify the consensus. They speak our words and express our thoughts, so we are expected to accept their judgment without further discussion, for now justice is being done.

In the consensus model we are expected not only to agree on norms and values and their interpretation; we are also assumed to agree that conflicts are unwelcome, noxious occurrences, threatening our social existence and our society, so that harsh measures must be taken against those who thus jeopardize the social balance. Unchecked conflicts might lead to anarchy. It is understandable that in a crime-control system relying so evidently on punitive measures, a well-empowered but otherwise well-controlled body should administer these firm and often harsh operations.

As a matter of course, if one thinks war is the ultimate way of solving international political problems, it is not a bad idea to institute a standing army and to establish it in a securely organized and well-controlled setting. If one adheres to the opinion that a war against crime implemented by a repressive system is the best way of coping with criminality, it seems appropriate to set up a standing, safely organized, and well-controlled body for criminal justice administration. The painful disadvantage of standing organizations, however, is that sooner or later they need to take action to prove themselves. Still, it seems a logical and watertight way of arguing. But is it a correct way of applying logic? Yes, if one accepts the premise.

It becomes a socially and ethically unacceptable argument if the premise is incorrect. And because the overall results of the repressive system are so blatantly unsatisfactory, one should have grave doubts about it. Criminality has never decreased as a result of repression; when it has decreased, the decrease was the result of political and economic factors and not because of the efficient administration of repressive justice.

Analyzing the consensus model a bit further, we find that the assumption of a firm consensus in society is not based on reliable research. It is rather an ancient, stereotyped way of thinking. Even in modern times, courts have rarely ordered sociological research regarding the normative values which they pretend to interpret in agreement with all people. In truth, this presumed consensus in the interpretation of norms runs counter to everyday experience. But in the consensus model such reservations are of no importance. For the model has become a persistent, quasi-metaphysical dogma and a logical axiom, not requiring further evidence. It is simply needed, not so much to maintain peace in society, for the model does not work and we have to live under an anomic system, but rather to give peace of mind to all those who find their work in the administration of justice. They would have sleepless nights if they thought their own work did not express the moral needs of the whole society.

What is the origin of this dogma, and why was it formulated? Since the Age of Enlightenment the consensus model has constituted a part of the dogma of the existence of a "social contract," the belief in some general agreement among citizens to cooperate for social benefits, e.g., by sacrificing some individual freedom in exchange for state protection.

In the course of the eighteenth century, as we have seen, trust in people's ability to resolve their own conflicts in a eunomic system of law gradually gave way to an exclusive system of state monopoly. Settlement of disputes was thus gradually taken out of the hands of the citizens, who in the course of several centuries unlearned little by little how to cope with their own conflicts. Their natural skills atrophied. The monopolized repressive system of crime control resulted in so much power being put into the hands of punitive controllers, and the abuses were so outrageous, that normal citizens could not as a matter of course be entrusted with such an intricate exercise of power. It seemed quite logical to allow a bureaucracy of more or less professional administrators of punishment to do the job. In the view of those who believed in the social contract, the citizens were quite happy to be relieved of the duty of resolving conflicts.

The consensus model assumes that the system of crime control is governed by strict rules and that criminal trials indeed solve the conflicts brought to them. But everyone knows that trials, like wars, do not solve conflicts, since they affect neither the cause nor the administered solution. Every war generates the germ of the next conflict, and every conviction implemented by the repressive system generates the germ of a new crime. But any such supposition is taboo in a consensus system; dogmatic doctrines are not supposed to be challenged. Many criminologists and well-informed lawyers may pronounce their doubts about its effectiveness, but the consensus model seems to stand firm.

On still closer scrutiny, the consensus model appears to be based on another assumption, rarely unveiled but as a matter of fact strongly felt by all participants. In order to serve the assumption of a social contract, our cultural system is believed to be composed of two layers: an upper culture and numerous subcultures underneath. This conception is a rather stereotyped construction of social reality. It can be compared to a similar conception with regard to language. Language likewise is believed to consist of two layers. At the top is the general civilized language, the received speech of cultivated, educated, well-bred, and civilized people. The people speaking that variety of a language are considered to be right-thinking and right-minded, having the right opinions about norms and values. They therefore are entitled to occupy the powerful positions, where morals are devised. In short, they are the moral entrepreneurs. The members of this culture are so self-assured that they often see themselves simply as *the* culture. But not everyone happens to speak, behave, believe, and act according to the norms and values of the upper culture. Daily experience shows that many groups construct different realities, acting apparently according to norm interpretations more or less at variance from those of the upper culture. How is this problem to be solved?

In a consensus model the solution seems easy. According to this model the concept of an upper culture is badly needed in order to weigh the variances of subcultures. Upper culture thus is believed to function as a sort of train schedule through which we get not only information about the departure and arrival times of trains but also about how far the trains are deviating from the schedule. A consensus model likewise needs an assumed upper culture in order to assess and control deviance.

In itself such a pattern of normative interpretation appears quite acceptable, but only if the upper culture is indeed a fair guide for the assessment of subcultural deviance. If all members of society without exception considered the upper culture as their own, supporting and helping them to shape their lives—if they experienced it as eunomic, serving all of them—it would be excellent. But reality is different. In general it is a subculture, not the upper culture, that provides people with eunomie. People experience eunomie if they can take part in the interpretation of norms and values, not if such an interpretation is imposed on them. But in a consensus model the division of upper culture and subculture unfortunately generates anomie.

The upper culture serves in reality as a subculture to those who actually have the power of moral enterprise. These powerful people experience eunomie because they know the ins and outs of their own culture. They seem amazed that members of other cultures become bewildered when strange moral interpretations are forced on them. If representatives of the upper culture could acknowledge that their interpretations are in fact subcultural, things might be better. But they cannot, not in a consensus model.

In particular the dispensers of justice behave like members of a subculture. They rarely explain their particular interpretations of norms, unfairly taking for granted that "of course" everyone knows what they mean. Since this pretended upper culture serves as just another subculture, though endowed with the power of enforcement, it contributes in large measure to alienation in society.

Eunomie can arise only when people partake in interpretations of morals concerning their own conflicts. Countries with the jury system should not be misled by the illusion of democracy assumed in this remarkable institution. A jury system of whatever kind by no means contributes to eunomie, since it is in all respects part of a punitive system and shares its anomic features. Jury verdicts do not settle disputes between parties or open the way to reconciliation and redress. A jury simply contributes to the repressive expulsion of offenders from society, to alienation of offenders and victims from their own conflicts, and as such it generates as much anomie as do repressive crime-control systems without juries. If a jury were a body of persons sworn to render solidarity to conflicting parties in dispute settlement, to accused and plaintiff alike, it might be marvelous. But the jury doesn't. The jury has been, since its very beginning, a lost opportunity. In the United States one even gets the impression that juries are intentionally selected to reinforce subcultural or racial tensions and thus to intensify anomie.

A consensus model is not only the determining principle of an anomic system; it is also its sting. Not only does it constitute the chief ingredient for the punitive model; it also produces the justification needed for disciplining mere deviance. When a consensus model is prevalent, the dispensers of justice create punishable deviance by labeling it as such, largely for the maintenance and continuation of their pain-inflicting bureaucracy.

The consensus model unfortunately has found support in structural functionalism. This sociological syndrome sees society as operating like a living organism. Consensus, according to this theory, is a pressing need of society, a necessity for the maintenance of the whole system and by implication for law and order. Any kind of conflict, any kind of deviance, might in principle constitute a danger for the social system. Therefore a workable social system provides itself with a servomechanism to prevent conflicts from arising; if they do nevertheless arise, a built-in and well-constructed institution becomes operative to eliminate conflicts and to make deviance innocuous. When social reality is interpreted according to a model of structural functionalism, survival of society is the highest pursuable value—and not just any society or a better one but rather the existing one. Any official action is justifiable as long as the system is kept hobbling.

We find several varieties of this kind of social interpretation in modern criminology. One is the so-called theory of social engineering, which holds that the maintenance of society should be realized, if possible, by decent and efficient means. Conflict should be prevented by effective servomechanisms that keep society in continuous balance by due measures at timely moments.

Usually, it is assumed, moderate measures of adjustment, if applied at the right moment, will produce a greater effect than harsh punitive arrangements badly administered and perhaps not accepted or internalized by society.

This sort of thinking does not seem unreasonable and is welcome to some. But social engineering is still very far from generating eunomic crime control. Under some circumstances, social engineering might even hamper eunomie, as long as it maintains a basically anomic system. Anomie does not become less objectionable if maintained by methods that should serve a better end.

We have an example in history: the "enlightened" princes of the eighteenth century. They wanted to keep their power upright by applying moderate, decent, but effective means and not by what they saw as the stupid harshness of their predecessors. But they remained authoritarian rulers. It might be argued that they contributed to the emergence of democratic movements in the nineteenth and twentieth centuries, but that is a matter of historical interpretation. Respectable methods of social engineering, if applied in a eunomic model, might indeed contribute eventually to the emergence of eunomie. But social engineering is not eunomie in itself, and it prepares eunomie only if certain conditions are fulfilled.

Another example is the concept of due process. It implies that fairness is offered by law and codes of criminal procedure, if only the requirements of the law are duly adopted. According to this concept, offenders get sufficient chance to defend themselves and to obtain fair trials if their lawyers and legal aid providers are willing to demand strict application of all the legal requisites.

The idea of due process is alluring, enchanting almost, if the legislator's original intentions had been to grant fair eunomic trials to everyone. But fair legislation, usually prepared by jurist-clerks, is not intended for all citizens, only for those who comply with certain conditions. These conditions include acceptance of the consensus model, for the decisions are made by the court and not by the conflicting parties; overall agreement of all justiciable participants to the consensus based on the existing procedural rules; their willingness and ability to speak the language of their prosecutors; and the means to afford lawyers who can get the court to observe all the legal technicalities. If offenders do not meet these conditions, no lawyer can help them. Thus due process, being the precise application of a wrong system of conflict control, does not lead to eunomie.

Due process may nonetheless have a favorable effect in the long run, for it may awaken people's interest in the necessity of rules, particularly rules of procedure. But it will help only if concerned parties, accused and plaintiffs, learn again to settle their own disputes, if need be by rules and procedures. Eunomie is based on rules known by and observable by the parties concerned.

It may be useful here to reflect on the remarkable expression "take the law into one's own hands." Where does the negative connotation of this expression come from? After all, it seems quite reasonable for people to take the law into their own hands. It is their law; it is everyone's law, and not just the repressive system's law. In reality it is the punitive administrators who take the law into their own hands, as if it were their property, while excluding the parties concerned. It is evident of course that the negative meaning of the expression originates from the simple fact that under a professionalized punitive system the concerned parties lose their skill in the proper use of the law. It would be better if the legal system taught people how to take the law into their own hands and to apply the law for a proper and fair solution of their conflicts. That would generate eunomie.

### The Dissensus Model

A dissensus model, in contrast to a consensus model, claims that regarding the interpretation of norms and values, the members of society never did and never will agree. Any assumption of such agreement distorts reality.[2] Given dissensus, conflict is conceived quite positively as an effective and necessary means for setting up discussions on the interpretation of norms and values, for contesting normative repression, and for safeguarding value-related interests. While the consensus model embraces the proud but careless assumption of general knowledge about good and evil, about right and wrong, the existence of such comfortable knowledge is disputed in a dissensus model.

Dissensus stems from an entirely different conception of culture. According to a dissensus model, all culture is entirely and exclusively built up of subcultures. Members of a society who call their own subculture the upper culture, or simply "culture," can do so only because, as a "top" culture, they are endowed with power to enforce their interpretation of norms on "bottom" subcultures. There are subcultures with and without such potentialities. According to a dissensus model, the subdued and oppressed bottom cultures should confront the powerful top cultures: this is the eternal struggle between top dogs and underdogs. Whereas power plays the important part in a consensus model, confrontation of power comes to the fore in a dissensus model.

From the viewpoint of social mechanics, the dissensus model is quite interesting. It shows a continuous tendency either toward a consensus model or toward an assensus model; otherwise it might end up in a sociocultural deadlock. If one of the disputing parties in subcultural disputes acquires sufficient power, it will try to enforce its interpretation on the others and thereby reach the status of consensus model. A dissensus model is a small-scale civil war, violent or nonviolent, between subcultures. Victory of either party leads to a consensus model. If the dissensus model tends toward an assensus model, parties come to some sort of fragile agreement that can be disturbed at any moment when old suspicions return.

If a dissensus model continues for a long time, it has a tendency to end in stalemate, for parties disputing along the lines of dissensus will try to organize themselves for the sake of survival. But then they will follow the destiny of all organizations: they will build up a bureaucracy, and all bureaucracy tends to perpetrate itself for nothing except the guarantee of jobs for the faithful.

A dissensus model in our culture is in fact more familiar than a consensus model, the latter being used only in anomic and repressive crime control. The dissensus model is most common in international affairs. It is particularly cherished by rulers of superpowers. When the Cold War was still going on, the superpowers often claimed to be champions of political values such as democracy and human rights. Their discussions usually had a propagandistic intent that allowed them to depict the opponent as evil and lacking all credibility. In a dissensus model one needs an enemy. This model is less common among nations on friendly terms with one another.

In many degrees of fierceness we find the dissensus model in our sociocultural system: in labor, housing, and armament, particularly nuclear arms. The means used in a politicized dissensus model are strikes, demonstrations, squatting, siege, occupation of buildings, barricades, etc.; these actions are meant to force the other side to discuss and negotiate. In recent times, ancient means of violent dissensus enforcement, such as hijacking, piracy, kidnapping, and hostage taking, have reappeared. They indicate a serious escalation of dissent. In a dissensus model the risk of escalation is always present, and sometimes even intended.

The ultimate aim of a dissensus model is civil war and eventual imposition of a consensus model by the victors. Citizens get fed up with aggressive dissensus and are, in their longing for peace, willing to submit themselves again to a political consensus model. But that will not last long either, except in the case of a dictatorship.

A dissensus model has been tried recently in the procedures of repressive criminal justice. Terrorists in particular have tried to use the model for their purposes. They have often succeeded in turning their trials into political dissensus arenas. They committed their crimes for political reasons, often using the same semantic tricks as their repressive opponents: they called homicide a coincidental casualty in wartime, or murder a popular execution, or bank robbery a confiscation or redistribution of wealth. Human semantic ingenuity is infinite. But semantic objections should be addressed to both controllers and terrorists.

The mischievous aspect of the whole thing is that in both models, consensus and dissensus, the participants seem to care nothing about the followup of crime. In a consensus model the administrators of justice inflict pain without much consideration for offenders or society, and they ignore the victims (plaintiffs). Justice in their narrow view is just retaliation for the crimes they have labeled as evil. Terrorists are by no means held responsible nor do they mind themselves regarding the evil outcome of their actions.

Dispensers of justice, whether they are public prosecutors, police, courts, or juries, pretend to have clean hands. As soon as the thorny subject of the followup of their pretended justice is raised, they look like children of innocence. It is not different with terrorists. I know of only one occasion when terrorists, during trial, spoke about innocent victims and offered to redress some of the hurt they had done to innocent people. They did so out of free will, not because the court demanded it. Punitive courts never demand responsibility and liability.

Does the dissensus model deserve serious consideration in matters of crime control and criminal procedures? Experience so far has proved far from favorable. The dissensus model is based entirely on political views; it stands or falls by politicization. It implies that crimes should be explained predominantly in political terms. Even if we grant that more criminality can be explained in political terms than many dispensers of today's repressive system are willing to admit, a crime is a crime. In a consensus model, politicization of crime is taboo. In a dissensus model, however, things move to the other extreme: most crime is considered political protest or the forgivable consequence of political action.

A dissensus model applied in criminal cases tends to be cleared away by semantic ingenuity. Even if all crime is called political action, the negative results of the crime are there, and they need redress. Political or not, anyone committing a crime must be held responsible and liable.

## The Assensus Model

The assensus model recognizes that full agreement with regard to the interpretation of norms and values among members of a society does not exist, has never existed, will never exist, and can therefore not be pretended either. In light of the human incapacity to make final judgments in matters of right and wrong, interpretations of norms and values must be made in a never-ending and open process of discussion.

In an assensus model emerging conflicts are transposed into dispute settlements between the parties directly involved. In crime cases, a reconciliatory redress in the postcrime situation is a mandatory subject of discussion.

The assensus model is not a relativization of matters of good and evil. It is most certainly not laxity in what is most important in human relations. On the contrary, in an assensus model the problems of right and wrong are taken so seriously that one is aware of our incapacity to pronounce final statements about them. In an assensus model one is suspicious of all final judgments: do not judge lest thou be judged. Most evil is the result of aggressive counteraction against evil. Just as most aggression is counteraggression, most violence is counterviolence, most punishment is countercrime, and most evil is counterevil. The original evil is abused to justify counterevil. But counterevil is as much evil as the original evil. It can come to a halt only if we stop applying evil, aggression, violence, and punishment, whether it be an original or a counteraction.

The fundamental principles of the assensus model have never been better analyzed than by Cardinal Newman. In *An Essay in Aid of a Grammar of Assent* he was engaged with the problems of faith and doctrine. He had a very practical and empirical mind, and that is why he wanted to establish the groundwork for human competence in ethical and religious affairs. In judgment, he argued, rules a twofold sentiment. One is the notional assent, which is purely conceptual, infertile, and often misleading. It is a kind of perceiving of reality that obstructs real cognition. The other is real assent, the positive and substantial accord to understanding and sensibility. Real assent involves the essentials of human existence; it needs the whole person.

All assent may have to be part of a long process, but in the case of real assent, interaction and adjustment are needed for it to come about. Assent is subtle and cannot be forced. It is generated by being with others as much as being by oneself. A community has to live with truth, to meditate on it, come to an affection with it, and learn to give it reverence. In the *Grammar* Newman uses what he calls the illative sense of meaning, a motion toward or into meaning. As an inference he states: I can prove Christian faith to my own satisfaction, but I can never force it upon someone else; assent is a body of grounds in their totality, although I cannot know all the grounds except by half-articulate experience.

Newman was a forerunner of the existentialism of the twentieth century, or, as far as the social sciences are concerned, of interactionism. All perception, all cognition, is always part of an interactionist process: we are incapable of any competence if we do not engage ourselves with other people as much as with ourselves. Cognition demands interaction, and interaction generates cognition.

Assensus is likewise the ground principle of the way in which Jewish people through the centuries have been dealing with Torah. Torah does not allow final judgment; it implies rather general directives, indications, road signs, invocations to discussion. Dealing with Torah is like taking a meal. We need food to stay alive, but taking food is also one of the major patterns of social interaction. We need sex, but having sex is likewise a major social interaction. Eating and having sex take place in our cultures in ceremonials and rituals, in old institutions as much as in arranged sceneries and playgrounds, but their social settings are as important as their biological, if not more.

So it is with law. Finding law, equity, and justice is a major pattern of social interaction. And the support of social interaction produced in the process of assessing law and justice is as important as the law itself. Is not the law there for us, instead of us being there for the law? Without social interaction in a reasonable and fair setting, there will be no justice. But what is a reasonable setting? The answer is not difficult: a reasonable setting exists when all parties directly concerned can interact.

In Jewish tradition Torah interpretation usually occurred in a *beth-ha-midrash*, a house of learning. This term speaks volumes, for Torah is not applied but is learned; Torah is not imposed but is pursued in an open and never-finished process. Some people are more learned in the law than others, but everyone is expected to take part.

We find a similar pattern of social interaction in non-Jewish traditions. In antiquity, justice was often discussed at the forum, the marketplace. All people concerned could take part in discussions about law, equity, and justice. That is the way to find justice, to pursue equity, and to arrange the problems of crime control.

We can see the assensus model all around us, in all our social patterns, all our interactions. Except in the present crime-control system it is omnipresent in the legal system, for the assensus model is nothing out of the ordinary. Unlike consensus and dissensus, assensus is the ground principle of our culture and our legal system. We practice the law when we shop, drive, discuss politics, vote, and settle neighborhood disputes. Though reactionaries might argue that people in modern society have unlearned to partake in law-and-justice interactions, the contrary is true. People are still as capable and eager in law interactions and discussions as they have ever been, notwithstanding the complexity of modern legislation.

Why has social interaction concerning crime control been taken out of our hands? Why is the modern criminal courtroom so alien? If juries would hold their discussions in the presence of offenders and victims, defendants and plaintiffs, then justice might be obtainable. It is a sickening delusion to speak of justice in the absence of the major parties. It is difficult to understand how an otherwise democratic culture such as ours could ever develop the ritual of criminal procedure that we now have. It contravenes all patterns of human experience regarding social life.

It is no better in the courtrooms of Europe where juries are either unknown or where just a few laymen take part in repressive decisions. The defendant may always be present in the courtroom, but the inequality in power between defendant and public prosecutor is so vast as to make justice unobtainable.

It is not that administrators of justice are unwilling or of bad character. "The senators are usually fine but the senate is awful," as the Romans used to say. The structures of criminal trial as we know them today, after erroneous development over several centuries, are unfit to generate justice of any kind. So many excellent representatives of the judiciary who could do a better job have no workable structures at their disposal.

Yet the assensus model is not all paradise. The great peril, always alluring, is power. People generate many mock justifications to defend their use of power. They argue that the only way to control power is to use counterpower, forgetting that the original abuser of power had used the same argument. So they are doing nothing but stepping into an escalation process. When the state received almost unlimited power, a monopoly of violence, using power against power, making the offender powerless, the result was not a balance of power, not even a control of power. The result was rather an overpowering force, so that normal human interaction was out of the question.

There can never be justice when the offender is made powerless. Justice does not endure powerless persons. Of course we are not justifying the offender. There is no apology for crime or criminal. But overpowering the offender does not result in justice.

## The Division of Power

Both committing a crime and repressing it are evidence of power. And we should not fool ourselves: in an assensus model, power cannot always be prevented; it might even jeopardize the whole pattern of fair dispute settlement.

Power cannot be controlled, let alone neutralized, by overpowering the powerful. That would just open the door for escalation. If we envisage a system of overpowering the criminal, as we do in the present repressive system, we run the risk that only the less powerful will be prosecuted and overpowered. That is inherent in the principal idea of power: all power yields to greater power. That is why the most powerful in our society can scarcely be overpowered by a power-based repressive system. A repressive system as a rule guarantees immunity to the repressors; if it did not, they could not do their repressive work.

A system in which the monopoly of power is granted to the state, as in the present unbalanced repressive system, does not work either. For if power is only on one side of the balance, fair dispute settlement is forever impossible. In fact, there is no balance.

Some people believe that power is a neutral phenomenon, its value dependent on its purpose and aim. Well-intended power, aiming at good, would be good; maliciously intended power, aiming at evil, would be evil. But that is an embarrassing fallacy, as long as the most powerful have the monopoly of defining good and evil. All good things can be polluted by the use of power.

We must avoid naiveté, however, and keep our eyes wide open. All the power, violence, and wickedness hidden or open in many crimes cannot be ignored. We are not dealing just with offenders and their victims; we are attempting to find the best way to cope with crime control. So we take crime seriously. People's fears of crime are real and must be taken into account. We must find ways not to escalate power and violence but to neutralize and eventually prevent them, for the benefit of better crime control.

## The Tripartite System

In eighteenth-century Western culture, the control of power was in the spotlight. It was even believed that the problem of power was on the verge of being solved. In many nations in Europe that had suffered from abuses of power since the coming of absolute monarchy, people were preoccupied with the control of power in modern state formation. As all the functions of political power had apparently been in one hand, people thought it proper to separate these functions and consequently build power control within the system of the state itself. A tripartite system seemed to be the answer. Legislative, executive, and judicial functions were to be separated; in this way they would eventually control one another. These power functions were believed to be already largely separated in England, and so the founding fathers of modern Western and parliamentary democracies thought it fit to elaborate on the English system in the most reasonable way.

But the aversion to absolute monarchy and the apparent success of the idea of division of power in the Age of Enlightenment should not make us close our eyes to the balance of power that existed previously. Emperors, kings, and princes in medieval Europe (France, England, and Germany) were far from having absolute power, as they had to share it with the nobility and the church. They were often bound hand and foot to either their lords or the good will of commoners in prosperous cities who had to finance royal warfare. Powerful kings often had to humiliate themselves in tours of entreaty for money. They constantly needed to seek coalitions. And later, in oligarchic republics such as Holland and Venice, all kinds of subtle power balances existed between factions. It has always been appropriate to neutralize power by power balance. It was not an invention of the eighteenth century, nor a particular English institution.

Between 1600 and the end of the eighteenth century, however, the original subtle balance of power had been disturbed. The political influence of nobility and church had shrunk considerably, and by gradually increasing taxation the princes had made themselves more and more independent of the cities. Thus in many countries an absolute monarchy could arise or power could get into the hands of a small ruling class.

At first sight a tripartition of power seemed to offer the solution. It was not a bad idea. The executive elaborates the laws given by the legislature, and if the citizens are dissatisfied they can appeal to the judiciary. Of course, in the past two hundred years we have noticed lots of imperfections in the tripartite system. We have discovered that power has gone to the captains of industry and lately to multinational corporations; we have seen the development of a huge caste of bureaucrats who sometimes seem to wield power beyond the law. But these developments are not the issue of this book.

Our focus of interest is the position of the judiciary. Again we must point to the "other side" of the Enlightenment. As a state monopoly of crime control gradually developed, it was better to have an independent judiciary as an authority for justice and appeal. But the judiciary, appointed by the executive, is not really an independent body; it belongs to the punitive system as a whole. And it guarantees the absolute exercise of the very problematic consensus model in crime control. The omnipotent system to which the judiciary belongs has stripped the citizens of their own conflicts; outside the system there is no salvation. So we can conclude that the tripartite system has not really abolished the dual or dialectic system of power balance in society.

### The Dialectics of Power

It is odd. The founding fathers of the modern state in Western Europe and the United States wanted to improve legislation. But in doing so they displayed an excessive confidence in the human ability to institute just legislation, unprecedented in history. One may argue that this confidence can be explained by the youthfulness of their constitutional endeavor; that many have believed that society can be ruled by good legislation; that law, if well given,

well observed, and well enforced, will lead directly to the ideal
state.

Before the Enlightenment, by far the greater part of the history
of Western civilization, confidence in legislation, interpretation,
and application of the law was less prevalent. Rulers tried to leg-
islate as well as possible; and while caring for the interests of their
subjects, they would, as a matter of course, not forget their own
interests. But in general people would usually doubt that others
could be ruled or controlled by law and law enforcement alone.
They were more ready to admit that law may always be deficient,
that the application of law suffered from human defectiveness and
liability to err. Briefly, they were aware that their legal system
offered only limited protection to people against abuse, corruption, profanation, and perversion of law. They were more prone
to realize that all endeavors to make perfect laws, though worth
pursuing, were doomed to fail because of human frailties.

The usual and time-honored solution to the problem of legal
imperfection was the presupposition of two legal systems, existing
and operating side by side. They supposed one system to be the
human system and the other a system beyond, either controlled
and exercised by God or simply based on the law of nature.
Although the idea did not find its origin in Christianity, the pre-
Christian world from ancient Egypt and Israel to the Greco-
Roman culture having known about it, the great master at the
analysis of the dual system of law was Augustine. In his *Civitas
Dei* he assumed the existence of two systems, side by side, operating simultaneously. One, the City of God, is the world ruled by
the deity. It is not a world of perfection but is a system heading
directly toward a world as God would like to see it. And, Augustine believed, this world will eventually pass into the end of times.
Alongside the Civitas Dei is the Civitas Terrena. This system is
also evolving toward the fulfillment of times. It is a system of
right and order on one hand but of disruption on the other. It is
not necessarily an evil system, just as the Civitas Dei is not a
world of pure good. Any assumed distinction between a spiritual
divine world and a material, secular world would not apply here,
either.

Augustine did not believe in dualism, for dualism was the basic idea of Manicheism, a pagan doctrine dating back to the Mazdaism of the ancient Persians, the belief that world history would display an everlasting struggle between good and evil, between God and Satan. Augustine believed he had overcome this dualism by the introduction of dialectics. For according to his opinion the two worlds need one another, presuppose one another. It is a deeply mystical thought, for all mystics have claimed that God is as much in need of us as we are of him. In the same way the Civitas Dei needs the Civitas Terrena, the latter having the duty to give law while needing the former to learn about justice and God's way with humankind.

One must understand the basic difference between dualism and dialectics. Dualism assumes the existence of good and evil, somewhat as in conventional western movies: good citizens and malicious criminals. Trivial dualism is not what Augustine had in mind. Dialectics is something different. It means that regarding the testing of truth, metaphysical contradictions, and opposing social forces, one side cannot be understood or even exist without the other side. Any difficulty or incongruity in one system can be counterbalanced by the other system. It is an interaction of systems, just as there is interaction of individuals. Nothing can be explained, nothing understood, without taking the dialectic opposite into account. Dialectic is the necessary and indispensable condition for all knowledge, for all justice and fairness, and for all equity and decency.

In the Middle Ages an understanding of dialectics, especially sociocultural dialectics, was still very much alive. It was easy for medieval minds to comprehend because they had a kind of dialectic model right before them: the natural division in society between church and state. They accepted the idea that Christ had bestowed two swords upon mankind, one on the pope and one on the emperor. But that is not exactly what Augustine had in mind. In his time the Roman Empire had just collapsed, and he could not predict that it would have a rebirth in a Frankish formula three-and-a-half centuries later. But there is still some correctness in that image. The highest ideal of the Middle Ages was indeed the appropriate balance between church and prince, a balance of power, a model of dialectics.

As far as justice and equity are concerned, the effects of such a dialectic sociocultural system have been enormous. For the idea implies that anyone, being adjudicated by one system and finding no justice there, could always appeal to the other system. It also meant two different belief systems, two different constructions of reality. "Appeal" did not as a matter of course automatically mean appeal to a higher court of the same system but could just as well mean appeal to a different system. Of course, vertical appeal within one system was possible, but so was horizontal appeal.

It is a construction we have not entirely lost. We find it in our international law of asylum. Persons having ideologies very different from those of the powerful in their own countries and therefore under threat of persecution may appeal for asylum granted by another state. In the medieval legal systems, horizontal appeal also took place inside territories. We cannot speak of territories of one state, of course, since the modern concept of the state did not yet exist. Europe was rather believed to constitute one single Christian empire, ruled by numerous princes; but inside that territory people could rely on two dialectically opposed ideal systems of law. Sometimes this meant that an individual could try to find the legal interpretation most favorable to him, but he could also try to find a better settlement of his dispute. And a dispute can be much better settled if one has a double choice of interpretation. It could mean that the individual would appeal to a visible dialectical power, the church; it could just as well mean an appeal to divine law or the law of nature.

The system worked wonderfully well. Dialectical control guaranteed to participants that neither could, ideally speaking, overpower the other. But at the beginning of the thirteenth century a very slow, almost imperceptible change began. That happened when the king (of France, in this case) began to use ecclesiastical law for the repression of unruly subjects (the Cathars). Ecclesiastical law used to be inquisitory and secular law accusatory; the two together made short circuit of belief. That was when our present system of criminal procedure received its baptism. It all gave rise to the eternal struggle in the Middle Ages between pope and prince and eventually to the substantial victory of the state. The church maintained its spiritual influence for another few centuries, until the Enlightenment and later secularism put an end to that as well. It is not strange that when the church disappeared as a visible alternative power, the notion of the law of nature also vanished. I don't mean to say that the church was ideal or was the expression of the law of nature, but rather that people had lost a model in their mind.

We should not forget that neither pope nor prince in the Middle Ages was exactly what Augustine had in mind. I have discussed the dialectical relation between the two as an example for better explaining what dialectics in a sociocultural and legal structure can and should mean. It might result in more legal security for the citizen, more equity, and more justice. Again, it is odd. The enlightened fathers of the innovative legal system of crime control around 1800 took pride in the thought that they had secured the equality of everyone before the law—real, legal security. But their contemporaries knew that the law is like a five-star hotel: everyone is equally invited to stay there, both rich and poor alike, but few do. Everyone today knows there cannot be even a pretense of equality; witness the hard fact that poor people and minorities are so largely overrepresented in prisons in all countries of the Western world.

Apparently the system does not guarantee a marvellous equality before the law. Who would dare to maintain stoutly that poor people and minorities are of a lower morality than the rest of the population? Any system of crime control can afford justice, or at least guarantee more justice than the present one, only if external control is possible, if two separate systems side-by-side allow the possibility of appeal to another system.

It stands to reason that I am not advocating a restoration of the medieval church and state. I am rather urging a complete reversal of the basic ideas behind the present system of crime control that have troubled us since the political revolutions at the end of the eighteenth century. The period's ideas on freedom and equality were wonderful, and no one should be exempted from them. Improvement of crime control needs a return to a dialectic structure of side-by-side power systems that guarantee justice to all.

## The Law of Nature and the Dual System

The idea of the law of nature has been an ancient, time-honored, fundamental part of legal philosophy and legal theory. The Greek legal philosophers exercised their minds to find a solution to the disturbing problem of the deficiencies in the human legal system. Injustice, inequity, and abuse of power being so blatantly noticeable in the world around them, they assumed the existence of another legal system lacking the deficiencies that worried them—a system from which we too may learn to improve our law. But where can we find it?

Some thinkers imagined that the other system could only be of divine character, some kind of spiritual law. Others hoped to find it in the nature of things, of relations and structures. Others argued that the law of nature was innate in all individuals, born within all of us.

For many centuries jurists and legal theorists, when pleading for a particular theory on law, referred to the law of nature, assumed to support their thesis. The "law of nature" could in fact serve advocates of any imaginable thesis on law. In the eighteenth century the theory of the law of nature lost its character of a belief system. More and more it developed into a rationalistic method of finding new law. Toward the end of the eighteenth century the overall confidence in rational legislation had grown so far as to make it unimaginable that any secular legislation could ever be against nature. A good and rational legislator was from then on believed to be capable of making laws entirely in accord with the law of nature. But if all legislation is per se assumed to be natural, the law of nature loses its function as a touchstone of justice. A given law and the law of nature become identical. No longer were two systems imagined to exist, but just one. The new thought was most conspicuously realized in the United States Constitution, and Napoleonic law, and in all the legislation influenced by them. The law was now considered to be good, and if any deficiencies or imperfections were left, a good legislator, inspired by parlimentary criticism, could improve that legal flaw without much difficulty.

All this led, as we know, to weird consequences concerning the natural rights of men. On one hand, men are believed to be born free and endowed with natural inalienable rights; on the other hand, many people still believe that the laws of nature can be suspended when human beings are being prosecuted by a "legal" institution. If natural law and given law have become identical, an appeal to natural law as a corrective for given laws is no longer possible. Nature cancels itself out if its laws can be suspended.

Throughout the nineteenth century and the first forty-five years of the twentieth century, confidence in legislation was so overcharged and extravagant that the belief in natural law seemed to have disappeared from the consciousness of humankind. That same era was precisely the period of overestimation of repressive criminal law. Legislators and administrators of justice no longer believed they could do any wrong and if they did, it could be easily corrected by better legislation. It was as simple as that. This overestimation occurred both in North America and in Europe.

Interest in natural law returned after legislators and rulers in Europe, during the Nazi period, perverted the entire legal system. If legislators and all given laws can become so corrupted, how can we establish moral standards for legislation? How can we trust law, and where do we find morality if not in a system beyond given law?

The omnipresent dictatorships before and after the Second World War created among critics a new awareness of the old natural rights conception of the rights of man. But as we discussed in chapter I, the notion of human rights today is still based far too much on the concepts of the Enlightenment.

It is remarkable that, in fact, the theory of the law of nature has never been a true dual system. The law of nature, from whatever source it was assumed to spring, always remained a belief system. Until the eighteenth century, when law and nature got identified, they were always a system one could believe in but not realize. For if it were ever realized it would merge into its double, and nothing of a dialectical nature would be left.

The system I advocate, following Augustine, is a dual system, believed to rest upon a dialectic relation. Anomic justice and repressive crime control represent one system, while a eunomic system of crime control and tsedeka justice represent the other. Eventually they might merge, but that would be in Augustine's fulfillment of time and most certainly not in our lifetime. If the repressive system of crime control could be brought under the dialectic control of a eunomic system, it might eventually lose some of its repressive traits, because it would no longer have the monopoly of prosecution.

## Why Retain the Present System?

It may seem strange, after the vigorous attacks I have launched against the existing repressive system of crime control, that I nevertheless recommend that it be kept intact. I do so for two reasons.

In the first place, maintaining the present system would give heart to the many people who fear violence. If the assensus model failed to work in a certain case, we could always fall back on the repressive system. The present system should always be kept in reserve, as a second string on the bow of crime control. It can never be said enough that an assensus-based eunomic system of control should never serve to explain away the seriousness of crime and the fears of the public.

But there is also a more social-theoretical reason to maintain the present system in reserve: we need the old system for its dialectical significance. We can deduce that from what has been discussed here concerning the dialectics of power. The only way to control power is to have a balance of power. If there is only one system of crime control, e.g., the existing repressive system, there are few limits to power. The exercise of such power obstructs justice and prevents a eunomic system of law from coming into being.

The same might be true if there were a single dispute settlement system of crime control. Dispute settlement in itself will certainly not guarantee the absence of power. One of the disputing parties, either plaintiff or defendant, might, if motivated by human malice, consider the abuse of power as a workable reality.

To obtain a balance of power, two systems must exist side-by-side. If two systems keep an eye on one another, they can keep each other in order. But the repressive system should be maintained only on the condition that it abandons its monopoly of crime control.

We should not forget that in former periods, when a system of dispute settlement was still in operation, the prince or any other power always reserved the right of intervention. In recent times, in many places in North America and Europe, the administrators of justice, though in full possession of the monopoly of crime control, have allowed some experiments in dispute settlement in cases of minor criminality. That is still far from being a balance of power, and compared to the dialectics we have in mind, it is but a minor step toward an assensus model. These experimental programs have sometimes failed because of their triviality; the concerned parties often have not been interested. Fortunately, many other programs have been successful, mostly in cases in which a wise district attorney has provided or worked with a victim-offender reconciliation program. Examples are the reconciliation programs realized by the Mennonite Central Committee in several places in Canada and the United States.

The dialectic balance of power will be realized only if the people involved have free choice to submit their case either to the old repressive system or to the system of dispute settlement. But the choice must be the litigants'; only in exceptional cases should the prosecution make this choice. The latter's monopoly must be broken. And the choice should embrace not only minor cases but also major criminality.

# 4

# DISPUTE SETTLEMENT

DISPUTE SETTLEMENT FOLLOWING crime is the attempt to create patterns of negotiation for the resolution or regulation of conflicts between disputing groups in order to transform repressive and punitive power into negotiative power, aimed at the eventual redress of harm caused by an offense. As a valuable part of crime control in our legal system, dispute settlement will be acceptable if it complies with these stipulations:

1. In a procedure of dispute settlement, disputing parties are not called offender and victim but defendant and plaintiff. They will, as a matter of course, discuss their issues only rarely on an individual basis. Real conflict resolution will usually demand the participation of groups: friends and relatives and, if necessary, providers of legal aid and social solidarity.

2. The issues under discussion during a procedure of dispute settlement will always be directed toward the need for redress of the harm caused by the offense. Guilt, blame, and reproach will be discussed only insofar as they are convertible to duty and can thus be neutralized.

3. Any state office will take part in procedures of dispute settlement only when it is in charge of controlling an equality of arms between the disputing parties. Only in the victimless crime cases will the state itself proceed as plaintiff.

4. Nonstate organizations will take part in dispute settlement to facilitate discussion, promote redress of harm, and draw up agreements.

5. Reconciliation between disputing parties is the ultimate goal of dispute settlement.

## Wrong and Abuse

Choice of terminology is of fundamental importance. What should we call the redress-demanding phenomenon? Crime, felony, offense, deviance, wrong, abuse?

Most people are caught up in a cluster of emotional associations of disgust, fear, and aggression as soon as the word *crime* is mentioned. These emotions are in themselves understandable and acceptable (though day after day they are exaggerated by news media bent on profit). That is why scholars in criminology and criminal law have tried to find new terms for this phenomenon.

*Felony* is a traditional term used to indicate grave crimes, but in its legal connotations it has ominous emotive consequences. In English usage it has a remarkable history. It comes from the Celtic word *felo*, meaning "traitor," and thus a felony was treason. When the state gradually seized the monopoly of crime control by defining crime no longer as an act primarily against a victim but rather a kind of treason against the state, the original meaning of the word got lost.

Clerks working on legislation later coined the term *offense*, a term likewise unsuitable for our present discussion as it carries with it all the notions of the present repressive system of crime control. When discussing a different system we must use a different term for clarity's sake.

Criminologists at midcentury, especially those scholars belonging to the so-called labeling school, began to prefer the term *deviance*. They too wanted to avoid the emotive connotations of the word *crime*, but they also had something else in mind. Their labeling theory put attention less on crime than on types of control and the management of stigma. They wanted to minimize the difference between crime and other types of behavior considered or labeled as deviant, such as homosexuality, drug abuse, and prostitution; because according to their theory the effects of social control differ little no matter which type of behavior is being controlled. All "deviants" are stigmatized. The great merit of the labeling school has been to point out that the social effects of stigmatization are often as bad or worse than the punishment itself and thus effectively worsen the injustice of the repressive system.

The labeling school, on the other hand has suffered from a frequent sociological inadequacy: its scholars have often been eager to describe and point out injustices of the system while keeping aloof from the search for a solution or the offer of an alternative. They therefore have made no contribution to the matter of dispute settlement. There is no advantage in using the term *deviance*, and I will avoid it.

I prefer the terms *wrong* and *abuse*. The first word, which lacks the emotive connotations attached to *crime*, points to the injustices people cause one another, injustices that need redress. What is "wrong" can be corrected, and that is what we are aiming for. I will apply the term *abuse* to what in traditional criminal law has been called a crime of order.

### Wrongs Causing Harm

In a repressive system of crime control it is not predominantly the resulting harm but the moral gravity of the crime that counts. The anomic system assumes that crime causes moral or social harm under the rule of law and under the structure of law and order, but the presumed harm has little or nothing to do with the real harm that has been caused. It is only fancied harm against the supernatural moral order. The real harm being of so little importance in the present system of control, many acts that are considered "offenses" cause no real harm at all. An example is homosexual acts between consenting adults, defined for centuries by criminal legislation as an "abomination" (the *crimen nefandum*, for people were not even allowed to speak its name). How many people who did no harm to anyone have had their lives ruined because of a charge of or a conviction for homosexuality? We find a similar predicament with regard to illegal drugs. Most drug abusers harm only themselves, and if their acts were not criminalized they would concern us no more than if they knicked themselves with a knife. Both actions are stupid, but should they be criminalized?

Punishment of crimes that cause no demonstrable harm, for the mere satisfaction of a moral principle, has been typical of law systems based on misunderstood monotheistic religions. A moral judgment laid down in some ancient tribal law has often been sufficient to punish people and thereby ruin their lives. Many highly developed cultures have existed, however, in which only real and demonstrable harm and not the moral value of an act itself gives rise to legislation. So if we turn our attention to demonstrable harm and call for dispute settlement, we bring our legal system more in line with the general culture on this globe— and also more in line with what the Bible originally meant.

If there is no real harm, a wrong is neither the law's nor the state's business. If defined as such, a "law of wrong" is going to look like a twin to the law of tort. This would be a fundamental change in modern Western legislation, for ever since the Middle Ages jurists and rulers have done their best to separate "civil/private/common" law from "criminal" law. They did so, as we have seen, in spite of the earlier Greek-Roman tradition in which the notions of tort and crime were not legally separated and in a way were even considered identical.

There has long been a fluctuating borderline between private law and criminal law. In eighteenth-century England, debtors were treated as criminals, and at times as many debtors were incarcerated as "normal" criminals (taking into consideration that a part of "normal" criminality was still dealt with by an assensus model and that a large number of "criminals" were actually Irish rebels fighting for their existence). The difference was in the treatment: criminals were incarcerated to be whipped, starved, and more often than not executed, whereas debtors could languish in prison while their means decreased and their debts increased—an absurd situation, for the creditors certainly could not profit from the ever-worsening financial plight of their debtors.

If demonstrable and provable harm is to be the main concern of a eunomic system of control, the perspectives are breathtaking. Until now, our system of crime control as a rule has accounted only for the moral culpability of crime, resulting in the cruel punishment of people consequent to the moral disapproval of their behavior, even if they had caused no real and provable harm to their fellow citizens. At the same time our system has allowed people to cause immense harm in political, economic, and socio-cultural interests without any accountability. The widespread occurrence and infrequent punishment of white-collar crime speaks volumes.

One can imagine some people objecting to the assensus model on the ground that if only harm counts in dispute settlement, some criminals might conclude that they could commit any crime if indemnification is paid. Some of these fears seem justified at first sight; rich people, after all, might commit crimes just for fun and then pay indemnification. But that type of argument can more readily be used against the present system, in which one can commit any crime one likes, arrest and no liability being the only consequence—if, that is, one belongs to the bottom rungs of society and is actually tracked down. Those belonging to the power structure of society runs less chance of arrest and detention, and many of them go free as a happy result of their social and legal skills.

In an assensus system one can also commit any wrong one likes, but the result is liability. In some cases, liability might strike the wrongdoer harder than punishment does, and there will be a greater chance that liability will also strike people belonging to the power structure. Wealthy people today resist being prosecuted because of the stigmatization which they fear might destroy their career, but they might more gladly contribute to dispute settlement.

### Abuses of License and Order

In the present system of crime control a clear distinction is made between crimes with a victim and crimes without. The distinction in the present procedure is more or less trivial, the victim playing such a small part in the trial, if any. In a eunomic, assensus-based procedure the distinction is more important, for if there are no victims, where is the demonstrable and provable harm?

In the repressive anomic system that question creates little difficulty. Victimless crimes are considered to clash with morality, implying the breach of a law or a decree and as such punishable. If the penalty is prescribed by law, no real problem seems to present itself. We see here the repressive system in its naked actuality:

human behavior being controlled and shaped by penalties regardless of the consequences of the penalties.

A breach of law without causation of demonstrable harm is in fact no wrong. If one makes a more than superficial analysis, the so-called crime of order is of an entirely different nature. It has usually to do with an abuse of license. Take driving. Even though many people seem to think that driving a car is kind of natural right, they are wrong. For since the very beginning of its invention, in order to drive an automobile one has needed a license, granted only under certain conditions.

The punitive urge in crime control often prevents legislators from taking the right legal measures in the case of abuses of license and order. If they become aware of some new undesirable activity going on in society, they may argue: "Let's deter the evildoers by punitive measures, fine or incarceration. We know that it does not help very much, but at any rate we have done something." It is, however, legislation based on embarrassment, not on insight into the problem. Suspension of license is a better measure than punishment, as long as the licensees know that they may lose their license in the case of abuse. Punitive measures are often based on legislative indolence.

### Political Crime and Political Violence

One of the most difficult topics of ethics, morals, and law is political violence. Imagine that some outside force (the Danes, for example) had come to the relief of the Saxons at Hastings in 1066. William might have been captured, indicted, convicted and sentenced for killing Harold, and executed as an impostor and regicide. But William was successful, and Harold's mother was even refused the corpse of her son. How do we define political crime and political violence? Violent rulers and their violent opponents, until the present day, have always committed atrocities against one another; but even in our Western democracies many of us are dupes of our own semantic ingenuities, which allow us to play tricks on one another.

Rulers have since the origin of human civilization tried to criminalize their opponents until the moment they were overthrown themselves. These criminalization procedures being so shrewdly achieved, a student in the history of crime control may easily overlook the fact that many crimes were often committed as violent political protest, while the archives simply define them as common crimes.

One gets somewhat tired of seeing the perennial struggle between rulers and their opponents who outbid each other in semantic ruse. Dictatorial governments are often more blameworthy but democracies cannot go free. The way rulers and their opponents treat one another is an inadequate training ground for better theories on crime control.

In the future, when an assensus model gets a better chance in our legal system, a more effective interference by parliament in the control of political violence may offer a solution. Reintroduction of national sanctuaries in a new form will allow the possibility of finding a solution to the problem. Political violence should be reduced to its major question: did the terrorists, these violent politicians, cause provable harm to other people or did they not? With respect to the harm they have caused, all actors in these violent political games should be as liable as any other wrongdoer, not only opponents but violent rulers as well. And since courts in a majority of countries are too much in peril of being controlled by rulers, an assensus model offers more prospect than present-day trials.

### State Organizations

Some degree of state organization in crime control cannot, for several reasons, be avoided. Even if the administration of justice were directed more along a tsedeka model, we would always need some kind of state control.

It is not so much the possibility of control that creates the problem here. The state should of course exercise control; why else would we have a state? The problem is its monopoly. As long as the state has the monopoly of crime control, anomic and repressive aspects will remain. If an assensus system is given a chance, side by side with the repressive system, both will control one another dialectically and the latter might become less repressive. If crime control is no longer monopolized by the state, its administrators will need to be more cautious in abusing crime control for the sake of political power. Participants in the assensus system, not having a monopoly either, will likewise pay heed to any abuse of power, for fear of losing the public's interest in dispute settlement.

A bipartite system implies that citizens have a right of option between two systems. They may choose not to participate in the assensus system. If offenders prefer to submit to a criminal trial, to spend their lives in prison without the prospect of reconciliation with their fellow beings and without settling their disputes, they will have a right to do so. But if wrongdoers prefer, together with their friends and relatives, to reconcile with others by dispute settlement, the state organization should not be allowed to preclude it except in cases of foul play.

Moreover, state organization of control will forever be required in so-called crimes of order, which I prefer to call abuses of license and order. These are disputes between the public representation and the abusing citizen, since the state as legislator and executive is here the plaintiff.

The courts cannot disappear either. They are needed in the remaining state system of crime control. But they may also play an important role if disputing parties in an assensus model are unable to solve their problems and need a sentence to extricate them from their difficulties. In an assensus model, though, the courts will only have a supplementary task. It might also happen that courts must intervene whenever an offender defaults on an agreement with the plaintiff.

Other state or semistate organizations such as probation services will not stay idle, either. With an assensus system in operation, they can assume excellent tasks in helping the system work when mediation, for example, is needed.

### Police and Police Investigations

When the assensus system of crime control still prevailed, a police force as we know it today did not exist. There were of course soldiers and city guards, and if need be they could be put into action to arrest people who were displeasing the rulers. Many a lord or sheriff had a constabulary at his disposal to hunt poachers and marauders, but as a matter of course the investigatory

force of these men was not very efficient and could hardly be
compared to modern police.

Ancient ways of investigation and arrest do not seem quite appropriate in modern times. Our countries have become too
densely populated and people's mobility too great. Nevertheless,
in the present repressive system only fools haunted by guilt feelings will as a rule turn themselves in to police. It is rather stupid
to do so, for the repressive system offers nothing but stigma: no
reconciliation, no possibility of redress, no way out. What would
motivate offenders to report themselves under the present system?

In an assensus-based system of control, in which wrongdoers
get a chance to settle the difficulties and to restore normal relations, the chances of self-reporting may be far greater. Self-reporting by a wrongdoer which leads to reconciliation with the victim
will have a far greater preventive effect as well.

We will most certainly still need police, but their tasks may be
far more satisfying. Under a new assensus system of control, the
police not only will conduct investigations but also will assume
the important task of facilitating dispute settlement. They will
need to refer both plaintiff and defendant to dispute settlement
localities such as neighborhood justice centers, arbitration committees, and the like.

We should not forget that in the not-so-distant past, constables
set up that sort of dispute settlement in neighborhoods. It was a
time-honored police task before the rise of the modern over-
technological society. Even today in the Netherlands, young police
recruits are told during training that dispute settlement in neighborhoods is one of their most important tasks. To their frustra-
tion, they get far too few chances to put this good idea into
practice once they are working in the field.

Police will also have an important task in connection with sanctuaries. I will discuss that in chapter 5.

### Public Prosecution and Its Monopoly

General remarks regarding institutionalized public prosecution
as it operates today are difficult to make because of the diversity
of legal structures and competencies in various Western countries.
In some countries there is hardly an office of public prosecution,

police being in charge of the practical prosecution immediately after arrest and lawyers in charge of prosecution during trial. In some countries public attorneys are elected; in other countries they are appointed like other civil servants and hold a rank in a stratified bureaucracy. In some countries the office of public prosecution operates under direct and permanent control of the minister of justice or the Home Office. In still other countries the office is almost entirely independent, responsible only to some high official within its own ranks. Most public prosecution agencies have arbitrary power to prosecute or not, according to some vague instructions. The citizens have control only subsequently, usually long after the event and through the medium of parliament or court complaint. Control following so long after the event, the harm usually has already occurred.

If an office of public prosecution or an attorney's office is lacking, as in some countries, that does not mean that the system as a whole is less repressive. It might even be a worse situation, as in the United Kingdom, where the absence of a public ministry has led in some cases to the conviction of accused persons without sufficient evidence.

The monopoly of public prosecution has been an erroneous development, and little good has ever come of it. Of course, given a repressive system, having a public ministry of prosecution is better than nothing, but still better would be a nonrepressive system of crime control. Then miscarriages of justice would be far less possible.

The power of most public prosecutors being so immense, abuse in cases of political violence is almost unavoidable. A major part of public prosecution power lies in its monopoly of carrying criminal charges before a court. If the prosecution wants to carry on a charge, nobody can stop it, except a court or someone at the top of the political administration. And if it does not want to prosecute, nobody can coerce it to do so, except a court or a minister of justice. The conflicting parties, victim and offender, or rather plaintiff and defendant, whose concern it is most, are deprived of all direct influence.

Arbitrary power is difficult to change. We might improve the situation a little if lawmakers could have far greater competence of control, most certainly in those matters where the political implications are quite evident. But again, the arbitrary power of the prosecution being so outrageously great, often matters have already reached a decisive stage before lawmakers get informed of the facts.

It might be worth consideration to include local councils in prosecution decisions. The policy of public prosecution cuts deeply into local affairs, and this policy is insufficiently controlled in most Western democracies. However, control of prosecution by a local or national representative body seems a better guarantee against abuse than the mere election of public attorneys. It is doubtful whether election of attorneys is conducive to a realization of the best issues for a eunomic system of law. As a way to a eunomic system, it makes little difference whether district attorneys are elected or appointed.

A major problem with the system of public prosecution has come to the fore in the last two decades. Public prosecutors have been complaining about heavy caseloads: increasing criminality, heightened control of drugs, new types of crime, increasing violence, greater pressures on the prison system. The complaint is well known, because the media are quick to inform the public about such things and the public attorneys like to use the media for their own ends. As an effect of this heavy work load, it is said, prosecutors must concentrate more and more on serious criminal cases, allowing minor cases to slide.

At the same time, active committees have expressed their intention to start programs of victim-offender reconciliation, participatory justice, and the like. Public prosecutors originally were delighted, as such programs offered a possibility of shifting prosecution of minor cases from overburdened public attorneys to these do-gooders. It has never been the intention of the initiators of alternative programs, however, to see their initiatives restricted to minor cases. Participatory justice in the future will be operative only if all cases, including major cases of violent criminality, are admitted to new programs of assensus justice.

In the future the monopoly of public prosecution should be neutralized by introducing a bipartite system of control in which an assensus approach has the same chance as the traditional repressive system of crime control. But the office of public prosecution might assume a wonderful new task in the future, when the assensus model gets its chance: that of pretorship.

## Pretorship

As we saw in chapter 1, the Romans were grand masters of law and jurisprudence. In considering reintroduction of a nonrepressive, eunomic, reconciliatory, and partipatory system of criminal law, we would do well to use some Roman ingenuity.

The Roman system of criminal procedure had a predominantly private character. Dispute settlement was in principle left to the initiative of a plaintiff or his kith and kin. That does not mean there was no state interference at all. As noted earlier, the Romans had a remarkable magistrate, the praetor, whose office we sadly lack in our modern system.

The tasks of the Roman praetor were quite different from those of the modern prosecutor. He was of course an administrator of justice, but unlike the modern prosecutor, his office was rather passive. Prosecutors proceed by their own authority and discretion, and neither victim nor offender can stop them. Both are submitted to the attorney's pleasure. The Roman praetor would not act unless either of the two parties involved asked him to do so. If crime was committed—say Sixtus stole a horse from Quinctus—the victim could not report it to police because there was hardly an institution of that name. If Quinctus knew the identity of the thief, he would try for a settlement. If the dispute could be settled with the offender, no legal action would be taken, unless one of the parties failed to stick to the contract of redress. The contract could be concluded either by reciprocal agreement or by arbitration. If Sixtus refused either to discuss the conflict or to proceed to a settlement, Quinctus as plaintiff could request legal action and suit, a so-called *actio furti*, from the praetor. As soon as a complaint was lodged, the praetor was no longer passive but would try to administer justice. He would adjudge arbitration and finally impose a contract by verdict, if he did not refer the matter to court for pronouncing sentence.

But the Roman praetor did more. As soon as the litigating parties lodged their dispute at his office, he could at any time interfere with the proceeding. His interference did not imply the assumption of a task comparable to the modern prosecutor, however, as he might still withdraw if both parties expressed the wish to continue their dispute on their own. But if they did not, he would, as president of a quaestio, attend the whole proceeding, taking care that rules were observed, paying heed to "equality of arms," and seeing to it that no party would overpower the other. Thus the Roman praetor was an equalizer, opening and concluding legal proceedings concerning crime dispute settlement. Nothing existed comparable to a common criminal trial except, as we have seen, in political cases. These were usually not the praetor's concern, his task being to ensure a fair dispute settlement.

A modern pretor? (And here I use the more modern spelling, without the *a*.) If we return to a bipartite system of crime control, we will also be badly in need of a magistrate competent in dispute settlement. Although an assensus model will not, like the repressive system, provoke only the bad character traits of participants, we still need proceedings control. As soon as a disputing party tries to abuse the situation and other means of guaranteeing equality of arms fail, some magistrate must be there to interfere and restore the balance of fairness. This new task of pretorship offers a pleasant alternative for those administrators of justice who fear they may become redundant when a bipartite system develops. From an ethical-legal point of view, equalization of dispute settlement can be a more honorable task than the present one of prosecution.

### Courts

Formal procedural traditions of Anglo-Saxon law concerning criminal procedures in England and its descendants in other English-speaking countries are different from the continental European tradition. The judge in English criminal law is far more passive, as this legal system applies in part the so-called accusatory system. On the Continent judges are more active, their role being based on a partly accusatory and partly inquisitory system. The differences between the two systems are of a predominantly formal nature, and their implications are usually exaggerated. Some traditional English lawyers tend to be proud of the accusatory system if it is compared to the continental one. But the difference lies in the fact that all the preliminary investigations are carried out by police, the judge usually being present only during the public trial. On the Continent a member of the court is as active in preliminary examinations as police and public prosecution, but the examining judge is never the same person as the judge at trial. The legal position of the prosecutee in both systems is equally weak, degrading, and alienating. In criminal trials a real equality of arms between prosecution and accused has never been intended.

There is little reason for English lawyers to take pride in their system. Neither is there any reason for continental lawyers to envy their English colleagues who serve as administrators of repressive justice. They all have just one aim in mind: to catch offenders, prove they are guilty, degrade them, then throw them into the destructive administration of incarcerative justice. Go to any courtroom in England or the United States and watch the everyday humiliations that take place as prosecutors and judges try to make a show of angelic innocence.

Still, if we ignore the abominable legal position of a prosecutee when in the hands of the prosecutors, the role of judge in the Anglo-American tradition is similar to what a judge's role would be in a system of dispute settlement. But in a eunomic system of law it would not be prosecutors and accused who appeared as the disputing parties before his bench but plaintiff and accused.

To understand better what is meant here we must give thought to the continuous struggle between Native Americans and the United States government. In the Native American legal system, courts and judges are as a rule unknown. Most conflicts are settled between disputing parties, with or without the advice of wise people and mediators. Having received advice, the disputants are free to decide whether they accept it or not, but they know nothing of enforceable court decisions or court arbitration. In their conflicts with the United States authorities, so often unfavorable to Native American interests anyway, the authorities always prefer an enforceable court decision because that has, in their system, more legal validity than anything else. Court decisions, whether favorable or unfavorable to the Indian cause, have always been a strange idea to Native Americans. And what made things worse, of course, was that white settlers took those court decisions or formal legal agreements even less seriously than the Indians did and simply occupied land wherever they could, without any kind of discussion except with their guns, usually provoking a new "Indian war." The conflict might have been interesting from a cross-cultural point of view had not the balance of power between the two been out of all proportion.

We can learn from this example. All things considered, a court sentence is alien to the procedural structures of an assensus system of dispute settlement, unless it comes as a last resort. Disputing parties take care of their own conflict and are not, if all goes well, in need of imposition of verdicts, let alone convictions. It might happen, though, that a court is needed if the parties are unable to reach an agreement and if mediation fails. Eventually, court mediation might be the only possible solution. But still, such mediation would not have the character of a criminal sentence but rather of a court order. One party might prefer to obtain such a court order with the intention of getting a more enforceable contract after settlement. But in that case the court decision would have the character more of a court's blessing on an accomplished agreement than of a sentence. Such details will be worked out when a system of dispute settlement is given a chance to develop. I must reiterate that courts will also be needed when one of the parties does not live up to the agreement at a later stage—and, of course, if the parties decide they do not want conflict resolution at all and simply prefer to fall back on the repressive system.

### Parliament

It is worthwhile to see whether parliaments might play a new role in crime control. It is remarkable how little is left of the ancient dispute-settling functions of parliament. The original meaning of the word *parliament*, from the Greek-Latin *parabolare*, is "a place where people can palaver," a meeting for discussing conflict, crime conflict included. Though the English word is of French origin, its semantic development followed an entirely different course in France and England. In France, parliaments remained or were later instituted as courts, and after the revolution of 1789 the word disappeared for the judiciary. In England, parliament continued to discuss conflicts but predominantly political matters and as such the word received international application. Its judiciary usage was reduced and restricted to those members of the House of Lords who were qualified to perform legal work. The French did not accept the "political" meaning of the word *parliament* as a national assembly because it reminded them too much of the old régime. And Americans have not accepted the word *parliament* either, because it reminded them of British rule.

If an assensus model of crime control gets a chance in the near future, it is worth considering a new function for parliaments (under whatever name: national assembly, congress, chamber of deputies, etc.), situated between political decision and judiciary: competence to take cognizance of political violence. The problem is not new. Many people fighting a political struggle believe that normal political channels have become insufficient for the repression of political violence. The blood of their "martyrs" is the seed of political desperadoes.

From the viewpoint of cross-time and cross-cultural analysis, it is interesting to see how again and again criminal courts stubbornly try to tell prosecutees that their political views are of no concern to the court, their violence being the only legal issue worthy of notice, while prosecutees try to tell the courts just as obstinately that their political struggle is the only issue worth discussing, their violence being a minor consideration. It is like a Ionesco play: nobody listening to nobody, but still a sad story.

The repressive judicial approach to political violence apparently has no effect, because political opponents using violence always find plenty of justification for their behavior in the violence used by rulers. Control of political violence by the usual criminal trial seems without any prospect of success, as both sides argue from a standpoint of power: who has the power to blame whom for political violence? In this case, power is the potency to criminalize others and to decriminalize oneself.

The criminal trial, so hindered by the dissensus model, is an inappropriate means for controlling political violence. Would a system of dispute settlement have a better prospect? Attempts by courts in the present system to make sharp distinctions between the political side of the occurrence and the criminal aspect are in themselves not objectionable. The difficulty is that the court is in charge of assessing only the legitimacy of the act; and because it must judge only the activities of the opponents, its decisions may lose a lot of credibility, turning into instruments of power and most certainly not of justice. Political aspects are ignored because the court is not expected to declare itself on such matters.

In procedures of dispute settlement regarding political violence, though, an essential new aspect receives consideration. Not the violent act but the question of harm is the issue for consideration. Having caused harm, whatever their political activity, the perpetrators would remain liable. But a similar liability would be borne by the authorities if harm has been caused by their violence. Both rulers and opponents would need to learn that violence, under tsedeka justice, always implies liability. That could result in more restrictions on violence than moral disapproval fosters. In dispute settlement, both parties concerned are accountable.

Parliaments in the Western democracies have for several centuries been the only state bodies meant to make political decisions. That is why a parliament should be competent to intervene in cases of political violence. Parliament should require from both parties, rulers and opponents, redress of the harm they have caused, and they should be allowed to dispute their case in front of parliament. When terrorists, for example, have redressed the harm they caused to victims, they could be just as valuable disputants as the rulers who have redressed the harm they caused. This proposal might look a little naive. But what are we to think about governments that hold such awesome instruments of power as secret police, intelligence agents, data banks, counterinsurgency bureaus, riot police, advanced armaments, and whole armies, but still stubbornly try to teach their opponents that violence is wrong? What happens is that the opponents of repressive governments also acquire similar armaments, which are freely available on the international market, often produced and marketed by the very country they are opposing. It is wise for a government to tell terrorists that violence does not pay, but it should begin by setting a good example. Violence breeds violence, regardless of who uses it.

## Nonstate Organizations

Crime control in our present repressive system has been the unique concern of state organizations. So far the state has obstructed eunomic criminal law rather than promoting it. A bipartite system, if allowed to develop, might bring a solution.

Some people favor the idea of an assensus model of dispute settlement needing no organization. They see any kind of organization as a fatal danger to conflict resolution. True, dispute settlement needs a far lower degree of organization than state crime control does. In the case of state repression of crime, the power granted to police, prosecution, court, and prison is so excessive and sweeping that a high degree of formal organization is needed to create an appearance of control. We know that such control is often fake, but some control is better than none. In a system of dispute settlement, balance of power and equality of arms are an essential condition, and a much lower degree of organization may be needed. But we do need some, for one of the greatest dangers in a dispute-settlement system is the possibility of power abuse between disputing parties. One of them, either by social and legal skill or by sheer abuse and blackmail, might try to put unfair pressure on the other. We need organization for the sake of equalizing procedural arms.

In recent years several scholars in the fields of cultural anthropology and social history have turned their attention to other cultures and to earlier stages of our own culture to find out how they settled their disputes and crimes. Criminal law in these cultures is much less separated than in ours from the other parts of the legal system. That explains why in other cultures people are less inclined to reach for criminalization if some behavior produces harm in their society. They seldom distinguish between tort and crime, as we unfortunately began to do in our culture centuries ago.

Nevertheless, turning to other cultures and former stages of our own remains a precarious tactic. Any reference to ancient institutions incites opposition from those opposed to legal change. It is not difficult to sum up their objections: these institutions might have been all right in other countries and ancient times and in very small communities, but in modern society they cannot be used anymore, or we modern people have become too numerous, too mobile, too complex, too alientated from one another and there is too much criminality. These objections are usually taken for granted and often highly stereotyped.

For a better understanding of cultural institutions in ancient times or different places, we need to follow the phenomenological method, in which an analysis of a phenomenon is accomplished by bracketing anything that is nonessential or redundant, particularly the peculiarities of time and place. It is true that when one studies historical facts and phenomena one runs the risk of making an anachronistic comparison. Anachronism is in particular present among the champions of punitive criminal justice who without further thought take for granted that all cultures in all times have had the kind of punitive and repressive laws that we have; they assume this to be the "normal" system of crime control.

If we propose to reintroduce an ancient institution in a modern form, we must indeed realize that modern society is quite different from earlier ones. A high degree of industrialization, internationalization, and mobility, though not ruling out reintroduction, nevertheless demand an institution in a form adapted to our time and place.

But there is no need to turn exclusively to ancient phases and other cultures for examples. If one has an open eye and a good theory, one will discover that our own society provides many institutions or social structures that with little or no change could directly serve in dispute settlement in cases of crime. If we redefine crimes as wrongs that need dispute settlement, we can proceed to apply several existing institutions of our present legal system for both new and ancient purposes.

### Assembly, Palaver, and Moot

*Palaver* is a Portuguese term meaning "word." By extension it means a place or an institution where people come together to discuss issues of interest. *Palaver* has become the general term to indicate "conference" and "prolonged discussion." Because people at palavers often talk at great length, the term has received a wider meaning of "profuse talk."

*Moot* is an old English word used in medieval universities when students were "meeting" to discuss hypothetical or logical problems. The word *moot* has been used by anthropologists in describing palavers they came across among several African tribes, particularly the Kpelle. Palavers and moots are still very much alive in parts of Africa, serving quite often in the settlement of disputes proceeding from crimes.

Palavers for dispute settlement are time-consuming and have a low degree of organization. One may argue that they are not very appropriate for a society in which time is money. In medieval and early modern Europe, before our culture became labor-ridden, people usually worked no more than ninety days a year. Much of their free time was spent celebrating holidays, such as those for local patrons and saints, but plenty of time was left for palavering. The time consumption was justified by its cultural and social value. As European culture evolved more and more toward a labor ideology, to the effect that the working class in the nineteenth century had to break its back 313 days in a year instead of ninety and seventy-two hours a week for the glorification of the new economic system, no time was left for palavers, let alone for dispute settlement. The new middle class thought it excellent that workers could no longer be distracted from their labors.

The already existing institution of public prosecution, which, though cruel, corrupt, and vicious, was small and almost marginal in society, now got the opportunity to make itself big and powerful. It dispossessed people of their own conflicts, telling them they could no longer waste their time on such futilities as dispute settlement. This latter institution did not disappear because people did not want it. They simply no longer had the leisure to cope with their own conflicts.

There is an interesting argument in favor of a revival of palavers and all other kinds of assensus justice. The twentieth century in the industrialized world has gradually displayed a labor evolution contrary to that of the nineteenth century. Whereas in the nineteenth century workers had to work more and more, in this century they have been working less and less. Particularly, automation has allowed for fewer and fewer working hours. People have time for palavering again.

Palavers are unstructured institutions of assensus and participatory justice, though in some cultures palavers are slightly structured: they are assembled at certain times, like the *ting* of the Germanic tribes. Tings were still assembled as late as the early nineteenth century in Scandinavian countries. Palavers usually work well in preventing crimes. Their function is to make clear to people that conflicts are theirs. If really difficult solutions are needed, palavers are inoperative. It is difficult to reach important decisions, and sometimes things get out of hand. No palaver should be allowed to devolve into a mob.

Many communities in the West these days have all kinds of citizens' initiatives with regard to crime: neighborhood crime watch groups, vigilance committees, semilegal militias with such names as the Guardian Angels. They usually arise when police tasks are neglected and are run either by people themselves in poor neighborhoods or by well-paid private security services in wealthy neighborhoods.

Although these initiatives are often the result of neighborhood talks, they rarely result in eunomie because they are based on deterrence of criminals and not on conflict resolution. Still, they reflect a beginning of awareness that we have in an unforgivable way neglected our duty of social control, allowing inner cities, for example, to fall into ruin.

First the modern state stripped its people of the possibility of solving their own conflicts; then it allowed the social control system to deteriorate; and now it tolerates a proliferation of anomic anticrime watch systems. The authorities should rather foster neighborhood palavers, where people can discuss conflicts and resolve them. It might be worthwhile to drop the term *palaver* and replace it with *assembly*, a term less loaded with unfavorable associations. But when the institution is once established, the right term will offer itself.

### Neighborhood Justice Centers

A neighborhood justice center (NJC) is the next step in structural organization. In a palaver, no special expert knowledge or sociolegal skill is needed or even expected. Everyone can take part in the discussions, and the expression of feelings and emotions concerning problems is expected and rewarded. But many conflicts are quite complex, and their settlement needs special skills.

An NJC may have any of several kinds of structure. A committee from the neighborhood with special gifts in settlement may be sufficient to reach satisfying solutions to difficult problems. For still more complex problems, greater skills may be necessary, those of a social worker or a lawyer; but NJCs should not become over professionalized.

Several places in North America and Europe have tried NJC programs in recent years. Some programs have not been successful, and the reason is evident. They could operate only as a favor of the official administration of justice, and they had to occupy themselves with cases shifted from overstrained police, public prosecutors and attorneys, who were allowed to select cases they thought suitable for NJC treatment while reserving to themselves the right of interference or interruption in the proceedings adopted by NJCs.

It is quite understandable, however, that the formal administrators of justice would wish to remain in charge and would feel obliged to control new experiments as long as the powers and duties of NJCs have not been statutorily defined. We still need detailed NJC legislation to safeguard human rights. We should try to enjoy the blessings of eunomie without falling victim to group coercion.[1]

### Advisory Panels and Mediation Panels

Advisory panels and mediation panels have been a natural part of our legal system. Whenever people have had problems, conflicts, or disputes, they have looked to other people for advice, counsel, and information as circumstances require. Such panels have a low degree of structure. Members are selected because of their special experience, training, and education. Those who seek their advice may accept it or not.

Advisory panels are among the most common institutions in our legal system, so normal and common that we are hardly aware of their existence. How wrong it is not to use them for dispute

settlement in crime control! They could have a great future as
valuable supplements to neighborhood justice centers. If social
workers and lawyers were allowed to be members of dispute settlement advisory panels, these panels could constitute the missing
link in neighborhood justice centers. In some ways they are already in operation in today's society, at women's shelters, for instance, and in houses for juvenile or psychiatric runaways. In both
types of institution, applicants receive help and advice without
being overpowered.

Mediation panels go one step further in structure than the
advisory panels. Whereas the latter may counsel parties in anything, the mediation panels try to intervene in disputes for the
purpose of reconciling them. In homes for battered wives, for example, we find women who would like to return to their husbands
if the beatings stopped. Often they apply for help to the staff of
the house. The staff, serving as an advisory panel, usually tells the
applicant that it would be better for her self-respect and assertive-
ness if she tried to resolve the conflict herself. If necessary, the
staff will intermediate, but only as a last resort and if both parties
want help. Mediation, like advice, is given without obligation to
any of the participants.

### Arbitration Boards

Like advisory panels, arbitration boards constitute a time-
honored part of our legal system. The structure is clear: if the
contending parties in a dispute have difficulty finding a solution
or coming to an agreement, they can decide to bring the problem
to a board of arbitration whose advice will have the force of law.
It is like a court decision to which disputing parties have agreed
to submit themselves.

In difficult cases in which the final decision will have a great
impact on the future of one or both parties, it is wise to seek not
only legal and social skills but also legal security. That is where
arbitration has its place. The arbitration board thus is one step
closer to the court system. Still, the difference between arbitration
and judicial verdict is great. In our present system of crime repression, neither plaintiff nor defendant has free choice of a court.
Even if both parties lose their faith in a particular court or be-

come doubtful whether their case is in the right hands, they have little chance to repudiate the judge or to challenge the competence of the court. We have the institution of contempt of court but not the institution of contempt of justiciables or contempt of contending parties, let alone contempt of prosecutees.

In the case of an arbitration board, both parties choose the judge. Thus as a matter of course they will be more disposed to accept and internalize the arbitration and to carry out its recommendations.

### Sociolegal Solidarity

The repressive system wears a weird coat of arms. Its blazon informs us that it is there to inflict retributive pain and injury on individuals and by incarceration alienate them from society. The results, of course, are disastrous. To make the outcome less threatening to society, assistance is instituted to see if some of the injuries can be healed again, not so much out of solidarity with the convicts as to prevent society from receiving too many misfits back from prison. It is condescending and patronizing; in short, it is anomie in its purest form.

Mental aid to delinquents maltreated by crime control and forensic psychiatry has been anomalous. Medicine in the Western world, according to the ideology of Hippocrates to which physicians still pay allegiance, is there to save lives and to heal people. Still, many psychiatrists in our punitive system have for 150 years been repressing people instead of healing them. When it comes to coercive therapy, many of these physicians forget the most sacred principles of their art. The best psychiatrists, of course, try to heal the mental harm which the repressive system has caused their patients. But the marriage of crime control and social or mental assistance has degenerated into the opposite of what was intended, into a sort of marriage between Heaven and Hell.

With regard to legal aid the situation is not much better. It is true that in modern societies people put on trial receive legal aid, paid for by the state if the defendant is indigent. But legal aid too is not directed toward dispute settlement.

Assistance given in cases of dispute settlement has rather a eunomic basis. It is meant to help people, not to get a legal advantage over them but to obtain a solution to their conflicts, to help them meet their duties and commitments, and to restore their spoiled relations. Assistance in such a system is meant to be solidarity with people who are faced with major life difficulties.

While the present probation and parole systems in many countries pretend to serve comparable purposes, their work is obstructed by the repressive criminal law system. Their cooperation with that system has made their efforts ineffective. They even tend to use blackmail tactics against their clients.

Assistance in a eunomic system is always offered without coercion: there is no obligation to accept it. The client is not treated like a child or a person out of control. Clients have the choice to fall back into the anomic system or to accept help and solve their conflicts. Solidarity is a feature of the tsedeka model of justice.

Let us consider some questions that might come up in administering solidarity assistance. Next to enforcement, professionalization has been one of the main threats to the credibility of social, legal, and mental aid in the present system. The more professionalization and specialization, the more power, and more power leads to more abuse and more alienation between provider and receiver. The system of aid developed in a eunomic system will keep professionalization down as much as possible. Disputes need to be settled by the disputants themselves: it is their dispute, and nobody should take it out of their hands. They will often be in need of help, both plaintiffs and defendants—and that is the difference: as in private law procedures, both disputants will need help. But their needs will always be of a mixed legal, social, and psychological character. Any professional who attempts to provide help should have an all-around training.

A major problem will always be equality of arms. A dispute settlement will immediately turn into a miserable display of human exploitation if the balance of power is ignored. Plaintiff and defendant should be admitted on equal terms during the settlement process. Careful legislation and adequate training are needed to secure equality. It will be the duty of the pretor to equalize the situation and to see that both parties get their rights, are properly esteemed, and are assured of proper attention to their interpretation of the case.

## Public Notaries

It is an ancient and honorable profession: the publicly author-ized duty to put facts, reports, rules of self-imposed obligations, experiences, opinions, and so forth into words, to record discus-sions, and to interpret conflicts so that contracts or agreements can be drawn up, attested, or certified in order to serve as law to disputing parties. On the continent of Europe the people who do this are usually called notaries; in other countries their duties co-incide or correspond with functions performed by solicitors, agents, advocates, or attorneys.

It is fortunate that in pleading for an assensus model in dispute settlement we have the example of the public notary, because it can serve as major evidence to substantiate the proposal that in general, most of our legal system should be based on the assensus model. The office of public notary is the standing model for what a public office in an assensus-based system of crime control can do. The notary is the assensus model incarnate. Whenever disput-ing parties lodge their dispute at a notary's office, they do not expect the notary to blame them for what has happened but sim-ply to help find a solution and then to put the solution into words that will rule out a future conflict if possible.

## Principles and Procedures

The procedures used in the familiar criminal trial in our present anomic and repressive system of crime control are vastly different from the procedures of dispute settlement in a eunomic system. Compared with a trial, the assensus procedure is almost another world. Nevertheless, dispute settlement is the most common and natural structure of our legal system.

The present criminal trial is based on three principles: indi-viduality, guilt, and punitive sanction. The principle of individu-ality implies that accused persons are defined, described, tried, and treated as individual persons, stripped of their normal sur-roundings and interaction patterns. They are socially naked, and their nudity is intended. The system wants the criminal act to be ascribed to the accused alone: if a criminal act has been com-

mitted by more than one person, individual ascription is still attempted, and the prosecutees must take care of their own defense,
without help from friends and relatives. A defending lawyer may
be friendly but is hardly ever meant to be a friend. Having too-
close relationships with accused persons might obstruct professional help.

The principle of guilt—individual guilt, that is—constitutes a
kind of mystical mark that sticks to individuals unto eternity.
Guilt, once assigned, outlaws persons forever; it deprives them of
most human rights and submits them without further defense to
any provocations which the administrators of justice, within the
limits of the law, impose on them, such as detention, incarceration, restraint, humiliation, degradation, deprivation of human
needs and comfort, loss of contact with friends and relatives—in
short, everything that belongs to normal life.

How little awareness society usually has of this remarkable
degeneration of our law can be deduced from remarks one occa-
sionally reads in the media. When journalists point out some maltreatment of accused persons or ordinary citizens, they often add:
"and this person has not even been tried yet and found guilty."
They seem to assume by implication that maltreatment as a matter
of course is legitimate if the criminal has been convicted. A trial
apparently opens the way to anything except . . . except what? Go
to any prison in the Western world used for preventive detention
and see what harmful acts are legally allowed against defenseless
persons. The mistakenly applauded "rights of the accused" may
sometimes prevail until the moment of conviction, but after that
they are nonexistent. And we have not even considered the many
thousands of persons in many countries who are locked up in
prevention centers or concentration camps, waiting for trials that
may never come.

As for punitive sanction, the outcome of a successful conviction
has always been the imposition of an injury. The character of
these punitive injuries has changed according to the fashion of the
period from physical harm to social harm to mental harm, but
conviction always implies suffering.

Eunomic, assensus-based procedures of dispute settlement, on
the other hand, are based on different principles, including the

liability of disputants; the opportunity for plaintiffs and defendants to argue and negotiate in groups, among friends, relatives, and providers of solidarity; and the assurance that disputes will remain open until a satisfactory outcome has been accomplished and drawn up in a contract.

Liability implies that both plaintiff and defendant, in their groups, must accomplish a redress acceptable to both parties in order to restore a situation destroyed by a wrong. It implies that the offender/defendant must perform duties to restore the former situation as much as possible and the plaintiff must accept the agreed duties in a reasonable way. Diminished mental accountability of the defendant usually does not remove liability but is rather an indication of the need for increased assistance to all parties concerned.

The enormous difference between guilt in the criminal trial and liability in the eunomic procedure is evident. Guilt is nothing but a mystical tie between an individual and a human act; it can never be removed. Liability is the natural outcome of a wrong committed and finds its culmination in the performance of acts during and after the discussion on dispute settlement. Liability can be controlled by the person it concerns: he or she can remove it by stipulated actions. Once fulfilled, liability is gone forever.

There is another major reason to plead for the concept of liability rather than guilt in crime control. Liability, in involving both disputing parties, is more or less the legal equivalent of the ethical concept of reconciliation. Reconciliation always needs the cooperation of both disputants. It takes two to reconcile. If one of them refuses to cooperate, no reconciliation is possible.

Even in cases of violent harm, when people have been violently victimized, both parties need to find a settlement. Some people might argue that this is an unjustified demand. In such cases the victim is often believed to be far too disturbed by emotion and disgust to participate in dispute settlement. Emotion and disgust in these cases are normal and acceptable, but why should they obstruct dispute settlement? Victims of noncriminal assaults such as natural catastrophes and wars are expected to stand up for indemnities and compensation for damages. Why should crime victims not be expected to do the same? Nonetheless, if they remain unwilling or unable, nobody should force them to defend their interests in person or alone. They can have themselves represented or surrounded by anyone they like, by loved ones or lawyers.

That brings us to the second principle of great importance in eunomic dispute settlement. It is not just the individual person who is involved; groups of persons around the plaintiff and the defendant take part in the discussions. We are by no means implying collective guilt but rather collective responsibility and group solidarity. The unconcealed injustice of our present system, in which a defendant is stripped socially naked, does not happen in a eunomic model. Here it is understood that the main figures in the dispute, plaintiff and defendant, may be less ready of tongue, perhaps lacking the necessary social and legal skills, whereas their friends and relatives may be better skilled in discussion. As a consequence, parties on both sides will always constitute a collectivity, a group, and never an individual. Groups can be made equal; individuals cannot.

The third principle of dispute settlement is its open structure. In the present criminal trial system the administrators of justice, not the plaintiff and defendant, control the situation. Opening and ending of the trial are entirely at the discretion of police, prosecutors, and court. Dispute settlements, having an open structure, in principle might continue forever. Parties can take their time, though time is never wasted. Discussions have social benefits, creating and promoting social cohesion. Dispute procedures allow people to work through their emotions.

It may happen, of course, that parties try to filibuster and obstruct eventual agreement. The problem is similar to what happens in parliamentary discussions, and the same measures can be used to prevent this.

### Structures of Procedure

Structures of procedure meant for dispute settlement are quite different from those needed for criminal trials. The major and essential condition is equality of arms. All procedures of dispute settlement should guarantee full equality of arms, with no possibility for any disputing party to exploit the other, to take advantage of any fact or condition outside the case that might eliminate or disregard the chance for a fair settlement. The fairness of dispute settlement depends entirely on this guarantee.

Another requirement of procedure in dispute settlement is freedom of negotiation. Unlike the plaintiff and defendant in a criminal trial, participants in dispute settlement are allowed to advance any argument they deem relevant for discussion. In palaver discussion, for example, disputants may refer to the behavior or activities of parents, using them as a valid argument in discussing redress. No severe judge or prosecutor is there to call the speakers down. Arguments may of course be rejected as irrelevant, but relevances are of a nature different from those in a criminal trial.

It is safe to predict that dispute settlement, if it gets a chance to develop, will evolve structures of a type with which we are already familiar in private law and international law. In general, three levels of structure can be distinguished: understructured procedures, half-structured procedures, and fully structured procedures.

Understructured procedures are used in many kinds of human gatherings: assembly, council, conference, parliament, synod, sanhedrin, convention. People come together to discuss issues of common interest, to get to know the general opinion, and to reach agreement and make decisions if possible. Sometimes nothing is fixed beforehand, the absence of prearrangements even being conditional to participation. For some gatherings a management committee prepares an agenda and formulates the wording of decisions to be taken.

As noted earlier, such understructured gatherings might be called palavers or moots. In its most unstructured form, a moot does not allow the precise designation of a plaintiff or a defendant (see figure I). An unstructured gathering would meet the requirements needed for a discussion of wrongs when it is difficult to point to one particular accused offender, either because he or she is unknown or because there are too many of them.

Cases of vandalism make a good example. The indictment and conviction of only a few persons makes little sense in these cases because the problem concerns the whole community. Everyone is a little bit guilty, for vandalism is usually the result of an exceptionally high degree of anomie in an entire community. People

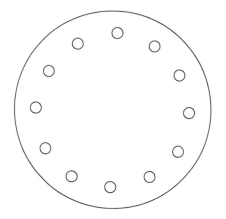

Figure 1. Unstructured procedure.

are no longer confident that the legal system works for their protection. The outbreak of vandalism in Los Angeles in 1992 is an extreme example.

Just punishment by criminal trial does not help. On the contrary, it affirms the feelings of anomie, making those convicted of vandalism sure that they were right after all. By applying repression the legal system gives overwhelming evidence that it is against them. Quite a few of the better administrators of justice are now aware of this argument, but the repressive system of crime control they must follow stands in their way. The system does not give them the tools to handle the situation, so nothing happens except mass arrests and mass punishments.

On the other hand, a palaver discussion in these cases would not ask who did it but what can be done. The main thrust would be to lower the degree of anomie.

In half-structured procedures for moot or palaver, the assembly is less dominant. Other participants serve as background to the disputing parties, who situate themselves right in the middle (see figure 2). A group around the plaintiff (P) and a group around the defendant (D) dispute the aftermath of the type of wrong: theft, burglary, mugging, or fraud. In the preliminary to the discussions, disputants agree that they will not enlist the services of the formal administration of justice. If the case has been reported

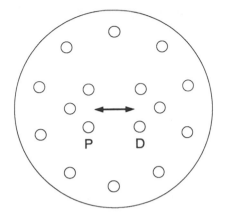

Figure 2. Half-structured procedure.

to authorities, however, the police may be welcomed to the discussions and even help in preparing them. As long as assembly discussions continue and both plaintiff and defendant are willing to negotiate, there is no interference by the formal system. Participants consider themselves capable of finding a solution. If need be, they invite as many friends and relatives as they want. If the problem appears too difficult or discussions flag, they may invite facilitators. They also may invite lawyers or social advisers to take part. Both parties may decide to continue until the moment has arrived to reach a settlement.

Eventually, in half-structured procedures the parties may come to recognize the need for a third, more objective person, a mediator. Mediation is friendly intervention or intercession between two persons or parties for the settlement of differences (see figure 3). Mediation will take place only by consent and invitation. Any mediatory intercession will never receive the force of law and needs to be accepted by both parties. A mediator is usually a person or group of persons chosen by the parties for their wisdom, knowledge, and experience. Both parties, after having accepted the advice of the mediator(s), may agree that the advice will be binding. But at the outset the binding character of the advice is not evident.

Mediation implies a many-sided activity. A mediator will take

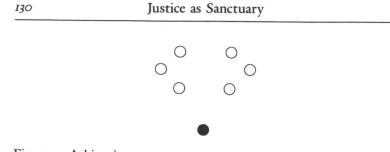

Figure 3. Arbitration.

all the necessary measures assuring equality of arms. The first intermediary advice may be to restructure disputant groups in such a way that inequality is neutralized or counterbalanced. The mediator may advise disputants to add more members to their groups or to remove some to facilitate discussion. They may advise disputants to invite more expert lawyers or a notary for the sake of formulating a better agreement or contract.

If disputants continue to feel uneasy, they may decide to lodge their case at an arbitration elsewhere. Arbitration is the settlement of a dispute by a person or a board chosen by free will to hear both sides and come eventually to a decision having the force of law for both parties (see figure 4). It is a structure that on the surface bears a striking resemblance to a criminal trial. Arbitration is in essence a type of mediation but is much more than mediation. The difference lies in the methods and in the effect. During arbitration procedures, just as in a trial, examinations and hearings can be quite common. The decisions of the board of arbitration, having the force of law, are executable, and refusal to carry out the obligations may have serious consequences.

Yet arbitration is wholly different from criminal trial. When seeking an arbitration procedure, both parties have, by exercise of free will, decided to lodge their case at the board; there is no arrest, no humiliation of the accused (because there is no accused), no loss of human dignity. Bail is replaced by another means of presence obligation, some kind of paroled presence at dispute settlement.

Some concomitant institutions of the criminal trial might be worth considering. The jury might be retained, though its task would need to be fundamentally reformulated. Instead of jurors

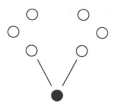

Figure 4. Mediation.

being summoned to help the judge in convicting and eliminating a prosecutee, they could assist in finding some solution before the arbitration board. It would be a jury of solidarity, sworn not to leave before a solution has been found assuring solidarity of jury and board with the conflicted parties in view of a performance of redress. The newly created pretor might assume the important task of equalizing the balance between conflicting disputants; solicitors might be needed to find the right formulations; and a public notary might be needed to draw up contracts.

Arbitration may have to take place in sanctuaries. Particularly if the dispute is on issues of serious violence and great harm, the emotions of people might be aroused to such an extent that a sanctuary would be the only place to guarantee the tranquillity needed to find a fair settlement. I will come back to that point in chapter 5.

## Redress, Reconciliation, and Reparation

All eunomic crime control must culminate in redress, the remedy or rectification of a wrong or grievance. If it does not, it has been a wasted effort. That is the great difference between an anomic system and a eunomic one.

In an anomic system the dispensers of justice are entirely satisfied in having the criminal duly punished and the prisons well filled. They live in hope that the nation will be grateful to them for having done a good job. In a eunomic system, all participants are satisfied only when equity has been restored, when a remedy has been found for the pain and grief the plaintiff suffered, and when the resulting damage has been rectified or repaired. In other words, a eunomic model of crime control must actualize what I have called tsedeka.

Still, redress is not the ultimate goal. Unfortunately, redress after a crime often is hard to achieve; frayed relations are not easily restored. The only satisfactory final result between conflicting parties is reconciliation, the only efficacious balm that heals real wounds left by wrongs. A wound caused by a crime can never be soothed or healed by punishment of the culprit.

The present repressive system of criminal law has resulted in an erosion of the concept of reconciliation, even in our legal language. When raised in legal discussion, the topic of reconciliation is often ridiculed. Yet reconciliation is the royal way toward peace of mind and peace in society. Reconciliation, though, is not a favor; it is not free. It takes time, work, and the solidarity of many people around those who need to reconcile. It is more than just repair, restoration, restitution, compensation, satisfaction, indemnification. It is a process of giving and taking on both sides.

The situation prior to the wrongdoing is hardly ever entirely reconstitutable. Here we become aware of the original meaning of forgiving. Forgiving is not the total acquittal of wrongdoers' debts. It is the acquittal of that part of their debts which they are unable to repay, that part of their due which they cannot restore, that part of their liability which they are unable to perform. Reconciliation is not possible if wrongdoers have not displayed their intention to negotiate redress and have not expressed their sincere regrets.

Reconciliation being the eventual aim of dispute settlement, it takes careful procedures of negotiation to assess the extension of liability for both parties. Not only must wrongdoers show their willingness to repair; plaintiffs must accept this willingness and forgive what the other parties are unable to perform. The process may take a long time, because the reality is that most people distrust one another. That is where solidarity comes in and remains of the utmost importance.

It may seem odd to focus special attention on redress and repair in a book concerned with crime control. But repair, restoration, and other such concepts have long been important parts of our legal system while being blatantly absent or simply accidental in our punitive system of criminal justice. In truth, the organization of repair is the main reason and justification for the existence of law and legal rules.

A system of restoration and redress instead of punishment sounds easy at first: the stolen object must be returned, the smashed object must be repaired, fraudulently acquired goods must be refunded, insults must be taken back. The catch in it is modern insurance. Insurance, if admitted into a eunomic system of crime control, might eventually undermine it. If the victim is insured against theft, who is going to be the plaintiff? The robbed victim or the insurance company? If it is the company, then the defendant will hardly ever have equality of arms.

Careful and scrupulous legislation will be needed to find a solution to this matter, on one side leaving the door open for a fair system of insurance but on the other not obstructing a system of redress. Reconciliation will work out only when the real victim is also the real plaintiff.

## Penitence

Many people favor the idea that convicts must do penitence for their evil deeds. But two systems of penance are possible. One is the penitence voluntarily assumed by the penitent, an act of benevolent display of the kind often done through religious pilgrimage in the Middle Ages, to reconcile with one's fellows in cases of violent and nonredressable crimes. The medieval penitent was rarely "sentenced" to pilgrimage, and even if he was, he still had the chance to accept or refuse.

The second possibility, the one used in our repressive penitentiary system, is condemnation to penance. That has nothing whatsoever to do with reconciliation. When convicts laid gas pipelines in the streets of Baltimore in the nineteenth century, they did no penance; they were convicts engaged in servitude, similar to those persons who were sold into white slavery in colonial America or the British convicts who were deported to Australia and the Russian chain gangs sent to Siberia. When penance is imposed and inflicted, it is immediately perverted into its diabolic opposite. Voluntary penance is the road to reconciliation if all other means have failed. Forced labor and imposed community service lead to nothing but humiliation, degradation, and labeling.

# 5

# SANCTUARY

A SERIOUS OBJECTION often raised against an assensus model of crime control is the presumed risk of self-help justice. If dangerous criminals are not immediately arrested and incarcerated after their crimes, the argument usually runs, the victims or their friends or relatives might "take the law into their own hands." That is a silly expression, of course, because the law belongs to the people, so they always have it in their own hands. But, it is feared, whole neighborhoods might get so outraged that they would start to hold lynchings. This fearful prospect bolsters the argument that detention not only prevents the criminal from committing other crimes but also prevents other persons from committing vengeful crimes against the offender. Arrest, incarceration, and conviction thus are justified by the need to protect both criminals and society.

Many experts in the field of repressive crime control who agree that the system is far from ideal nonetheless see no other solution in view of the risk of self-help justice. They might be willing to believe in the suitability of dispute settlement for minor crimes, even to accept reluctantly this model for crimes of the medium range, but they will usually stick to the opinion that we need the repressive system for the control of crimes that arouse emotional outrage. Anything is better, they will argue, than allowing people to administer revengeful justice on their own authority.

The argument, so seemingly obvious, must be taken seriously. But is it justified? Is it based on experience and hard research or is it just common belief? The argument is so frequently raised by rote as to arouse suspicion. Where is the evidence?

The origin of the belief and the major source of would-be evidence can only be found in history. In medieval Europe and in some countries as late as 1600, especially among the nobility, blood feud was an accepted legal institution. Members of a slain man's family had the right to get revenge by killing the slayer. It was a legitimate institution, but subject to often strict rules and conditions. If the slayer and his friends, relatives, or family displayed a willingness to negotiate on a possible solution, the right of blood feud was reduced accordingly. If the slayer sought and found asylum in a sanctuary, nobody was allowed to kill him in revenge, or even to touch him. (The old meaning of the Greek word for "asylum" was "untouchable.")

Since many countries were studded with sanctuaries—in principle, every church, temple, or other sacred place or locality could serve the purpose—the quarry would most often elude the vengeful pursuers, and they had to content themselves with dispute settlement. People realized that a blood feud could, as a matter of course, easily get out of control and escalate. Because any revenge beyond equity balance would allow a counterfeud, the case could eventually develop into a civil war. Thus negotiation and dispute settlement were common, punishment rare, and revenge unusual. I prefer to call that period the age of dispute settlement rather than the age of blood feud.

The argument that people would begin lynching criminals if there were no arrest and subsequent punitive justice is based not only on inadequate historical knowledge but also on myth. The barbarity of lynching, so prevalent in the United States after 1865, had nothing whatsoever to do with crime control. It was the ominous, violent, and criminal racial suppression of the African-American population by a dominant white majority enjoying impunity. African-Americans at that time were unable to defend themselves against such violence, the justice system being on the side of the whites and often in their hands. Thus the argument is inappropriate in our discussion.

Nonetheless, lynching has happened, and it can happen again. People get emotionally excited; they panic and may lose control. We cannot expect all people to remain cool and dispassionate in the wake of violent crime. Emotionality can make them unable to talk about what happened, let alone to settle the dispute. In such cases sanctuaries guarantee to both offender/defendant and victim/plaintiff a period of cooling down to prepare negotiations and reach a settlement in tranquillity.

## The Right of Asylum

Asylum is the protection from arrest by some authority guaranteed to a refugee by another authority. The meaning of the word *asylum* in Greek is "no right of seizure." The right of asylum has always been a firmly established institution in our legal systems. At present its best-known use is in international political asylum, the shelter and safety guaranteed to a fugitive from one state on the territory of another state. The fugitive has usually sought refuge on political grounds, being most often a political opponent of the rulers in his or her own country.

Political asylum has a glorious history. The granting of asylum to opponents has been viewed by rulers sometimes with gnashing of teeth when their prey eludes them, sometimes with joy because they are delivered from an embarrassing nuisance and are no longer under the obligation to prosecute them. Rulers have often tried to diminish the right of asylum or to promote stricter international rules on its applications. But their endeavors have seldom been taken seriously, for many rulers are aware that they themselves may one day be obliged to seek asylum somewhere. Often they make political money out of granting asylum: it is the game politicians and rulers like to play, and they understand one another all too well.

A sham difficulty often cited when political asylum is discussed concerns the protection it grants to the authors of political violence. But hypocrisy is the order of the day here, for persons who use violence to attain their aims often commit the same kind of violence that rulers and their aides commit. Terrorists on one side may be called freedom fighters across the border. Our semantic lust has no limits.

The number of asylum seekers has increased dramatically in recent years. It is caused on one hand by the availability of more rapid transport and on the other hand by the availability of much better information about nations or locations believed to be favorable to asylum seekers. Also a factor is the ever-increasing difference in wealth between nations: the far too rich and the far too poor. It is understandable that wealthy nations would attract greater numbers of asylum seekers.

But asylum has a broader aspect. Originally asylum meant protection from arrest by a ruler on one's own territory. Not only sacred places but also diplomatically warranted locations have long enjoyed, and still enjoy, immunity. Embassies, often to the embarrassment of the ambassador and his or her government, regularly grant political asylum. In Afghanistan recently, even the office of the United Nations served as asylum to a former ruler. An interesting development.

From a legal point of view, an embassy does not belong to the territory of the host nation, so in a way it can still be considered a place of international asylum. But what about churches that grant shelter to political refugees in many American countries? These are remnants of the ancient practice of internal asylum. In antiquity and during the European Middle Ages, internal asylum was quite common and generally accepted. Egyptian pharaohs granted the right of asylum in temples. When Julius Caesar conquered Egypt he reaffirmed this right of asylum to avoid difficulties with powerful priests. Anglo-Saxon kings granted the privilege of sanctuary in many churches.

Internal asylum was based on a particular view concerning the legal system. As already noted, this system was perceived as dual, ruled by a dialectical relationship between the two parts. Justice and equity were commonly assumed to be unattainable through one system only. Appeal of a judgment or sentence of one system could be found in the other system, which might perchance apply different rules. For a time the church served as the dialectically other system, as indeed canon law used to be different from the secular one. Canon law was not perceived as having a higher status, even though some popes might have liked it that way. Inherent in the dual system was the idea of divine and human law. Secular law often being too imperfect, too deficient, for granting ideal justice, it was expected that nonsecular, or natural, law would guarantee equity. The attractive idea behind this duality is that the dialectic tension apparently offered better warrant for eunomic justice.

There were as a matter of course more reasons for this prospering internal asylum and the sanctuaries in earlier periods. Europe itself during the Middle Ages was actually considered to be one empire: the realm of Christianity. Going abroad meant in fact going to the territories of the infidels, the Saracens in the south of Spain or in the Orient, or far away in Asia. Precisely in view of poor transport and difficult journey, this Christian territory was immensely large. Fugitives could not always go to the Saracens and Moors to find refuge, and so they needed and found internal asylum nearby.

## Sanctuaries in History

### Antiquity

A sanctuary is the visible location where the right of internal asylum can be realized. The English term *sanctuary* reveals the ancientness of the concept. A sanctuary used to be a holy place where a fugitive was regarded as a protégé of another authority, usually of divine nature. The deity was believed to protect the locality. The sacred nature of the locality conferred a certain inviolability on a fugitive, who was made holy by religious associations and therefore untouchable by worldly powers.

Sanctuaries undoubtedly date back to the origins of human civilization. Caves with prehistoric drawings may be explained as sacred places where fugitives tried to invoke help from the spiritual world for their protection. Later, the sanctuary was a firmly established part of all ancient legal systems, including Mosaic law.

There were to be six sanctuary towns in ancient Israel, according to the law of Moses. Such sanctuary towns were often exempt from direct secular jurisdiction, to be ruled by priests or other sacred persons; they were often sort of temple towns. Mosaic law stated that all fugitives—all those prosecuted, persecuted, pursued, or hunted, regardless of the political or nonpolitical aspects of their actions, whether debt or wrong—could find refuge in sanctuaries. Slayers particularly would find shelter, as they were most in need of it in view of the possibility of blood feud.

There was one interesting exception: no shelter could be given in cases of premeditated murder. That is important, because this restriction turns up again and again in legislation concerning asylum through the centuries. This restriction can be found in most documents granting the privilege of sanctuary by any secular authority in any sacred place. It is doubtful that the restriction has ever been of much selective value, though. It has always been difficult to provide evidence for premeditation. Between entirely unintentional homicide and premeditation lies an extensive gradual transition. Premeditated murderers might well have taken the possibility of escape into consideration and might not need sanctuary. Quite often, premeditated murder is a perfect crime, thought to be an accident or a mysterious disappearance. Unpremeditated murder, on the other hand, occurs most often as a sudden impulse or when a fight gets out of hand, so the slayer has not taken the precaution to prepare escape or to suppress the evidence. The main reason for the exclusion of premeditated murder from the right of sanctuary may have been the far greater barriers it presents to reconciliation. Persons who have committed unintentional manslaughter have a greater chance of convincing people of their repentance than does a conscious killer. Sanctuaries usually demanded a willingness for reconciliation from the fugitive.

Sanctuaries in antiquity were multipurposed. As stated in Mosaic law, they served as shelters to all those being prosecuted or persecuted. In Egypt the temples offered refuge to fugitive slaves, although they were obliged to work for the temple. Their lot may have been better in a temple than in their former servitude under a master, but the temple apparently offered no freedom—except that the slaves could always run back to their former masters.

Sanctuaries in antiquity were often large places, sheltering persons of all shades and varieties: political dissidents, rebels, fugitive prisoners of war, persons deviating from the official creed and opinion, debtors, and of course criminals. If the sanctuary comprised a really large area, such as a township (free town, *ville franche, Freistadt*), overcrowding probably was no great problem.

Some temple areas in Egypt numbered more than forty thousand inmates. Those who did not work for the temple might run their own small businesses or practice a craft. In large localities the pressure on refugees to seek reconciliation or dispute settlement with their prosecutors may have been fairly light, but in smaller localities the threat of overcrowding probably created extreme pressure on the fugitives to find some solution that would guarantee their eventual departure. In larger localities the fugitives often had their families living with them.

The most important aspect of sanctuaries has been their preventive effect, far greater than that enjoyed by today's jails or places of preventive detention. Even if no reconciliation ever resulted, sanctuaries nevertheless offered an immediate chance for a better life. In the Jewish tradition, the response to the question "How do we know if our sin has been forgiven?" was "When we are no longer committing that sin!" It is not through punishment that we learn to abstain from sin, but from the awareness that we are sinning no more. Sanctuaries offer a far better route toward that end than do prisons. But prisons in antiquity were practically unknown. Slaves and other persons without status, for example, could be held in custody without trial, but not Roman citizens. The prison as a penitentiary institution was unknown.

### The Medieval Period

When Christianity became the dominant religion in Europe and the Catholic Church the sole recognized religious institution, the existence of sanctuaries created no problem. On the contrary, the firm belief in a system of divine law found in sanctuaries one of its most visible and established practices. Pagan temples, transformed into places of Christian worship, continued the privileges they had always enjoyed. Many churches and newly founded cathedrals, minsters, monasteries, and abbeys demanded from kings the privilege of granting sanctuary, which for them was a distinct sign of their identity. Anglo-Saxon kings regularly granted rights of asylum and sanctuary.[1] Many privileges of sanctuary granted to churches and abbeys in England date back to the eighth century. Often the granting of sanctuary was not even demanded by a particular sacred locality, as it was assumed that this privilege would naturally attach to it.

Medieval rulers did not see crime fighting as their particular task. The existing system, though not perfect, satisfied the need for crime control, and dispute settlement happened to be the citizens' and not the prince's business. It is true that the Norman and Angevin kings tried to impose public prosecution on England—and succeeded partially—but they did so more for political reasons, such as policing and dominating a subdued but still unruly country, than for crime control. Not until the sixteenth century did rulers really began to worry about what we know as crime control.

The myth about sanctuaries has gone so far that in present-day English the term *sanctuary* has received a secondary connotation of a place where everything is allowed, where people can freely commit all kinds of evil without punishment or control. In the media one might read or hear sentences like "the police force today is a sanctuary for all kinds of psychopaths to do as they like," or "you can't do that here, you're not in a sanctuary." Myths have usually an obstinate vitality; they die hard and can only be neutralized by revitalizing and sensitizing the original meaning.

We do know a lot about some places of sanctuary. A well-known sanctuary in medieval England was the Minster of Beverley in Yorkshire. A minster, or monastery, was more than just a church building. It usually comprised a rather vast precinct, with many monks and other inhabitants. Beverley was granted the privilege of sanctuary in 927 by King Aethelstan, the first Anglo-Saxon to rule over the entire territory which today is called England.

Several signposts outside the town of Beverley indicated the distance a fugitive needed to travel to reach the sanctuary. Two of these signposts were still there in 1992. The right of sanctuary began half a mile from the actual precinct and was indicated by a milestone. From that milestone onward, the fugitive could no longer be arrested; anyone who made an arrest there would forfeit a fine.

In the middle of the fifteenth century, a period of turmoil surrounding the Wars of the Roses, about two hundred persons a year sought and found sanctuary in Beverley, most of them because of manslaughter. That is about four a week—a large number, in view of the fact that England at that time had no more than three million inhabitants.

Refugees could stay in the minster for one month on condition they were willing to settle their dispute with those who were after them. Prosecution was carried out either by private persons seeking revenge or by public prosecutors. During this first month the refugees were considered guests of the minster, and they took their meals at the canon's table. If after one month no agreement had been reached, they could stay another month but had to eat in the kitchen. If after the second month they had still not been successful, they could stay a third month, but now they had to work in the garden and contribute to their own sustenance. They also had to continue to show willingness to negotiate with their prosecutors. If after the third month of negotiations no settlement had resulted, there were two possibilities. Either the monks would take the fugitives to the coast and put them on a boat to the Continent or, if another safe place was available, they would grant the fugitives safe conduct. Sometimes fugitives stayed in the minster and worked there for life. It appears, however, that most fugitives succeeded in settling their disputes within three months.

Beverley Minster is the proud possession of one of the three frith stools (sanctuary chairs) known in England. The other two are at Durham Cathedral and Hexham. According to tradition, King Aethelstan would have bestowed the stool to Beverley. The stool is an armchair of hewn stone, very cold to sit in. Today the Beverley stool stands beside the altar. The actual function of the frith stool is still under discussion, and it seems to have had variable functions. The stool is said to have been the symbol of asylum, and anyone reaching it and sitting in it could no longer be arrested. In view of the usually longer stay of the fugitive in the sanctuary, a permanent stay in the stool must have been a bit awkward. The other function may have been that any prelate would pronounce the formal grant of asylum to the fugitive from the stool.

Noteworthy in this connection is the meaning of the old Anglo-Saxon word *frith*. It is etymologically the old and general

Germanic word for "peace" (German *Frieden*, Dutch *vrede*). The word has the connotation of a horizontal relation. It has a meaning different from the modern word *peace*: it is peace resulting from dispute settlement. When Norman rule was established over England after the conquest, the new kings introduced the Latin word *peace* in legal language. This term has far more the repressive meaning of vertical relations, the king's peace.

Other medieval sanctuaries probably functioned much like Beverley. It is in the nature of things that medieval rulers were not always elated to have sanctuaries in their realm. It was not about crime control that they worried but rather about political opponents and rebels in their territories. Still, they rarely dared to have a fugitive dragged out of a sanctuary. Violation of sanctuary, even by a king, was considered a great crime.

### The Early Modern Period

Rulers began to make endeavors to abolish sanctuaries in the first half of the sixteenth century.[2] Henry VIII's chancellor Thomas Cromwell did his utmost to make sanctuaries illegal in England. The motive was not crime control, however. Henry and Cromwell were concerned because Roman Catholics were seeking sanctuary from enforced Anglicization of their churches. Henry having declared himself head of the church and defender of the faith, it was a defiance of his power to grant his subjects refuge and immunity in what he now considered his churches. Henry's actions sounded the death knell for sanctuaries in England, though their total disappearance took a long time. The idea of sanctuaries stayed alive in England until the middle of the eighteenth century.

A well-known example is an area in London off the Strand, near the ancient Temple. This Temple, like the Temples in Paris and other European cities, had never been a real sanctuary. But when their owner, the Knights Templar Order, was dissolved by the pope at the request of the king of France and the pope bestowed most of the order's real estates upon a newly founded sovereign Order of the Knights of St. John, later the sovereign Order of Malta, many Temples henceforth served as "embassies" of the Knights of Malta and as such enjoyed immunities.

The Temple in Paris was used as prison for Louis XVI, and from there he was taken to his place of execution in 1792. In that same year the French revolutionary convention succeeded in what the powerful kings of France, swelling in their absolute monarchy, had never been able to achieve. The convention abolished forever in France the right of asylum, with the following words: "The right of asylum is being abolished in France, for it's now the law being the asylum of all people." A more naked statement about the abolition of the dual system, so honored before, but also about the new conception of law in the Age of Enlightenment, has perhaps never been pronounced.

The Temple in London lost its function as a Maltese "embassy" under Henry VIII and became exclusively the "sanctuary" for London barristers, solicitors, and jurists. But for centuries people remembered the earlier function of the Temple area and continued to claim it unofficially.

A remarkable example of the sanctuary function is found in the free towns in the Netherlands, which prospered during the Dutch republic, between 1580 and 1795. Several towns had received a reputation as sanctuaries even before the Reformation, but when the Reformation came, after 1579, the religious functions of the church buildings changed. The new Protestant doctrine no longer implied the permanent presence of God in a particular place; according to the new doctrine, God was believed to be present wherever his name was invoked. People soon realized with great dismay that they had lost their sanctuaries. Several ancient secular sanctuary towns thus began to prosper, taking over the former sanctuary function of the church buildings. Crowds of people annually sought refuge there until 1798, when sanctuary rights were abolished. The idea and the institution of sanctuary were not in agreement with the new legal ideas of a state monopoly of crime control, established in the Netherlands that year.

Recent historical research has found that two main categories of fugitives came to seek sanctuary in these free towns: debtors and slayers. Before the nineteenth century, any insolvent debtor, in particular after bankruptcy, was in a risky position: bankrupt debtors were always suspected of fraud; it was believed that insolvency would have been impossible if they had been honest. In

England debtors were incarcerated—until death, if they could not pay their debts. In Holland incarceration for debts was rarer, and debtors, fraudulent or not, often sought sanctuary and then tried to settle their financial disputes.

The two most famous free towns were Vianen and Culemborg, just south of Utrecht. The legal position of these places was complex. The Netherlands at the period had a weak federal government. Both Vianen and Culemborg were counties, not having even the provincial government as their overlord but some count or earl, and later the prince of Orange. Particularly the successive princes of Orange tried for centuries to increase their power, and one of the ways they did so was by insisting on the acknowledgment of their rights of sovereignty, which included the right to grant sanctuary. They not only maintained the right of sanctuary but also afforded letters of safe conduct to those trying to find refuge in Vianen and Culemborg.

The story of a city of sanctuary in Denmark is fascinating. In the seventeenth century, Prussian power was increasingly threatening the borders of Denmark. A reliable way to fortify the borderland was to build new bulwark cities, so King Frederic II founded a new town in the south of Jutland, named it after himself (Fredericia), and tried to populate it rapidly by granting it the privilege of sanctuary. Religious dissidents (Roman Catholics and Calvinists in this case, for Denmark was Lutheran), debtors, and slayers were granted asylum. Within a few years the new town had several thousand inhabitants. The privilege of sanctuary was not abolished there until 1827, when Denmark too gave in to the new ideas on criminal legislation.

## Objections to Modern Sanctuaries

Some persons object to the reintroduction of the right of sanctuary, feeling that it would fundamentally contravene our present legal system. As the argument goes, sanctuary without direct consent of the authorities would be in open violation of the law. Sanctuaries would be invaded and all their inhabitants arrested at the first and best occasion. Sanctuaries, according to this argument, would be tolerated by the authorities only if they regarded them as a convenient part of their criminal policies.

The argument, however reasonable at first sight, is but a partial truth. If we analyze our legal structures and the ins and outs of our legal system quite carefully, we will discover that reintroduction of sanctuaries would by no means be contrary to the fundamentals of our laws. Two main points sustain our thesis: there are many loopholes in modern legislation which might allow internal asylum and, in any case, such asylum is still an integral and essential part of our modern legal system.

Loopholes in the law became a point of discussion in the 1970s when foreign workers in several countries were threatened with expulsion from their host countries. During the years of prosperity they had served well, often doing in the industrialized world the unpleasant jobs which the autochthonous population did not want to do. But when recession hit, the authorities were quick to seize the opportunity to get rid of them, to declare them illegal residents if possible and threaten them with expulsion. These poor people looked around for help and recalled the ancient sanctuary privileges of churches. Many sought and found refuge in places of worship. Congregations usually reacted with surprising hospitality, even when the foreign workers belonged to a different creed. The Christian congregations felt ashamed of the merciless attitudes of their authorities, and here we see how the often deservedly repudiated overemphasis on culpability teachings in Christian doctrine might have its positive aspect. All of a sudden the ancient custom of granting sanctuary was revived: the foreigners lived for some time in church buildings, undisturbed by police and prosecution, and from their places of refuge negotiated with their prosecutors. To their pleasant surprise, they often succeeded in delaying their expulsion until the courts had an opportunity to occupy themselves with the legal aspects of the problem and to pronounce their findings. Often the rulings went against the authorities and the law had to be adapted to the new situation. The sanctuary movement was born.[3]

What made the authorities shrink from invading the churches? What made them shy back from dragging the refugees out of their shelters, taking them to a police station, and forcing them into the first and best means of transport outside the country? In most of the cases the authorities felt constrained by emotional situations; it was difficult to oppose entire congregations bewildered by the attitudes of their own government. But even more they realized the awe-inspiring respect for places of worship. Even in today's modern society these places exercise a numinous influence, and it is simply considered wrong to enter them by force of arms. The instances of refugees being dragged out of churches by the strong arm of the law remained small in number. Nevertheless, opinions among the congregations were sharply divided. Some became joyfully aware of the church's ancient function; others considered this function entirely obsolete, a jeopardy to good relations between state and church.

Remnants of laws on internal asylum are in force today. In the codes of criminal procedure of some countries, (the Netherlands, for example), we find paragraphs prohibiting any arresting officer from entering any location generally devoted to religious worship while services are being held. In principle a congregation that starts a religious service but never concludes it would by such an act create a legal place of sanctuary. All things considered, though, such a paragraph is but a thin legal basis for beginning a sanctuary experiment. Sanctuary would most certainly still be entirely dependent on the tacit permission of prosecuting authorities. If their power was in peril, they would enter the new sanctuary in spite of the law.

In Europe and North America the Roman Catholic Church no longer claims this right, apparently for political reasons or perhaps because the church too has been influenced by the idea of the state's monopoly of violence and crime control. Only in Latin America is the church's prerogative still kept alive. The right of sanctuary apparently is respected even by most barbarous rulers, perhaps because they themselves might need it one day.

We now come to our second point: that internal asylum is still an integral and essential part of our modern legal system. A close look reveals several clues suggesting that the idea of internal asylum accords with the general principles on which our legal systems are based. We can even argue that internal asylum and sanctuary should be viewed as fundamentally supporting our rule of law.

In many countries, especially those adhering to parliamentary democracy and the tripartite division of power, the law apparently prohibits arrest not only in places of worship during religious services but also in houses of parliament, other buildings of public assembly, local councils, halls of justice, and other premises used in the formal administration of justice. Arrests in such premises can be carried out only by the guards serving the premises on the special order of the chairman or president of the assembly or court. All these places lie outside the warrant of district attorneys and in fact outside the competencies of any public prosecutor.

Is it absurd to conceive of a hall of justice as a sanctuary (though some people might rather see it as the lion's den)? Immunity of such a premise guarantees not only the undisturbed administration of justice but also the prosecutee's right to receive eunomic justice. Considering halls of justice as sanctuaries might also protect future defendants against any abuses that might arise during dispute settlement procedures.

It stands to reason that if sanctuaries are reintroduced into our system of crime control, they should be based on a legal statute. Authorities should be prohibited from making arrests in any premise privileged to serve as a sanctuary, except perhaps by special order or warrant of a court. And it should not be necessary to open sanctuaries in breach of the law. Sanctuary should be considered a constituent part of our legal system, and all we need to do is to claim it for new immunity localities serving dispute settlement.

Halls of justice are not the only example of immunities in our legal system to which we can refer. In recent years there has been a revival of the sanctuary function of embassies. European and North American embassies all over the world are continually confronted with the problem of asylum in their embassies. Examples of embassies serving as refuge in recent years are plentiful.

Meanwhile another model of sanctuary is emerging. Modern mobility and the attractiveness of rich nations to inhabitants of poorer countries results more and more in mass attempts at illegal immigration. Many international airports have some kind of se-questration area that serves as a reception center for refugees. These centers allow immigration authorities to find out whether applications for asylum are based on economic or political grounds. In some countries these centers look like prisons, but in fact they are not. Sequestered persons can leave whenever they wish, on condition they leave the country. Thus, in a way, sanctuary is foreshadowed here. A defendant in a sanctuary also can leave at any moment.

It seems clear that the institution of sanctuary can be an integral part of our legal system. Embassies may serve as the best model for legal regulation, and we can learn from this model how future statutory rules concerning sanctuaries should read in order to guarantee a system of dispute settlement for both violent and nonviolent crimes.

## Modern Sanctuaries

Before examining questions surrounding the establishment of new sanctuaries, I need to state exactly what I mean by the term *modern sanctuary*. A modern sanctuary is a place of immunity and refuge where fugitives from prosecution, persecution, or revenge by legal authorities or any other power can be secured against arrest or violence on condition that they contribute to negotiating a resolution of their conflicts.

In earlier times the privilege of sanctuary included rules concerning the internal and external legal position of the premise. Most of the rules concerned statutory prohibitions against refugees' carrying arms into the sanctuary, general injunctions to open negotiations for dispute settlement with private or public prosecutors, and stipulations concerning the term of accommodation in the sanctuary. Quite different rules applied to large sanctuary areas and small ones. For example, rules concerning the term of stay were stricter in small areas, whereas some sanctuary towns allowed long stays. Some of the old rules may apply equally well to modern sanctuaries, and we can learn from them. But society has undergone fundamental changes, and many ancient rules may be inappropriate.

## Categories of Refugees

What sort of persons can we expect to seek shelter in a modern sanctuary? The least problematic group would be illegal immigrant laborers. In many countries the law is not entirely unfavorable to illegal inhabitants, allowing them to appeal unfair or illegitimate treatment. But the wheels of the law often turn too slowly for their protection. Authorities in charge of controlling foreigners often confront the appellate system with an accomplished fact, and the illegal inhabitant has been transported back over the border before the decision of the court has been pronounced. Particularly if the foreigner is a person of poor means, it is often too late, even if the court decision is in his or her favor. Sanctuaries would be extremely functional in such cases: a highly necessary supplement to the legal system and the rule of law. It is surprising that sanctuaries have not already been set up for this purpose. Nonetheless, establishing sanctuaries for this category will be difficult. Rich countries tend to close their borders to economic immigrants, and in view of rapidly changing political and economic situations, it is impossible to predict what will happen.

Another category of refugees will be those who have committed wrongs and thereby aroused the emotions of their victims or the revengeful compulsions of a neighborhood. We have considered their case in chapter 4 and elsewhere in this book.

In recent years we have witnessed the rise of places of refuge for runaways from psychiatric hospitals and for battered women who have left their violent partners. These are real sanctuaries, either tacitly tolerated by authorities or, for battered women, protected by authorities. Experiences acquired in these places will be extremely valuable for the future establishment of general sanctuaries.

The most difficult category of refugees will be the violent rebels, or, as they are usually called, terrorists. It seems proper that they should be allowed entrance only if they are unarmed. But it may be that even after authorities become willing to tolerate sanctuaries, they will make an exception with regard to terrorists, who pose a threat to the power of the rulers. Proponents trying to open sanctuaries may need to go along with such requirements if they are made a primary condition. But terrorists in spite of their desperation should eventually obtain the same possibilities of refuge that all other fugitives receive. Terrorists often are people of great social skill, and they might be able to help other sanctuary residents resolve their disputes. At the same time, they might learn the lesson of how to resolve conflicts by negotiation instead of using violence.

### Management

Concerning the management of sanctuaries, we have already acquired some relevant experience with houses for runaways and battered women. There should be a domestic staff, of course, to take care of the daily needs and supplies of a sanctuary. Residents too can help, but continuity is important.

More intricate is the question of legal aid, social aid, and aid in dispute settlement. Professionalization is a great risk for sanctuaries. As soon as professional providers of aid are formally organized, they tend to bureaucratize themselves; that seems to be a fundamental law of organizations. If this happens with fugitives, they might fall from the frying pan of repressive justice into the fire of professional and bureaucratized dispute settlement. The staff serving a sanctuary should never be allowed to develop into a professional team of aid providers.

Residents in sanctuaries should help one another, calling upon professional aid only if their own efforts fail. One main goal of sanctuaries in the new legal system will be to stimulate the innate capacities of people to occupy themselves with their own conflicts and to settle their disputes in their own ways. We should not allow a new agency to relieve them again of these fundamental responsibilites.

### Large and Small Sanctuaries

Experience has taught us that it is not always satisfactory for people with similar problems and belonging to the same category to live together for a long period. They tend to overstate their problems and even to develop querulous behavior. Getting a taste of problems different from one's own makes a person look at life in a better perspective. It can be quite instructive for refugees to compare problems and the various possibilities of negotiation. These observations suggest the preferability of large sanctuaries.

There is still another important argument against the small sanctuary. As we know, being prosecuted has a labeling effect: people tend to stigmatize fugitives from the law. The same effect could result if we have special sanctuaries for criminals, other ones for illegal residents, and different ones again for runaways. A fugitive staying in a sanctuary renowned for a particular category might suffer from stigmatization.

What is a large and what is a small sanctuary? We know from experience that a small church building does not work. If people are going to stay in any locality for some time, they need water, hygienic facilities, a kitchen, and beds. Monasteries would fit the purpose quite well. Some are no longer used for religious purposes and have been changed into motels or hostels. Why not keep their original sacredness intact and make them into sanctuaries? Certain urban areas might also fulfill the purpose, if they can be isolated from other areas. But a sanctuary cannot be so large that residents cannot keep some control over their own population.

In this instance we cannot learn from history. Society has changed too much for us to be sure whether larger or smaller sanctuaries are preferable. We must learn from experience.

### External Relations and External Authority

A sanctuary should never be allowed to become a secret or closed place. Civil authorities have the right to know what is going on inside. All fugitives should report their arrival to these authorities. Residents have nothing to hide, for the attempt to resolve a serious life problem should not be a shameful undertaking. They should have the chance to prepare openly and frankly for dispute settlement. Fugitives who refuse to report their arrival to the authorities may be asked to leave the sanctuary. There is good reason to maintain an open attitude toward civil authorities. Any sanctuary must endure suspicion, and it will only get worse if the sanctuary withholds information about what is going on inside.

### Relations with Public Prosecutors

A sanctuary may be thought of as an embassy for persons who are subject to prosecution or persecution. And for the legal structure of sanctuaries we may properly take as a model the statutory provisions concerning diplomatic immunities. Police are not allowed to enter an embassy unless invited by the ambassador, and that happens only rarely. In periods of international tension, police maintain the immunity, keeping a close watch and sometimes placing guards around the premises. Similarly police could keep a close watch on a sanctuary, controlling persons entering and leaving. Special arrangements and understandings would need to be worked out between police and the staff of a sanctuary concerning their mutual relations and rules governing the entry and departure of residents.

Relations between sanctuaries and district attorneys will need to be of a sophisticated nature. We must distinguish carefully between wrongs and abuses. If a wrong causing harm is the basis of the dispute and there is no violence, a sanctuary is not the place for dispute settlement, for this can be implemented anywhere.

In violent crime cases the sanctuary is the proper location. In an assensus model, however, the only really acceptable disputing party is the plaintiff, not a public prosecutor. If disputing parties can agree in a fair way, it is no one else's business. If after prolonged negotiations the parties still fail to agree, the sanctuary will have to decide the case. The fugitive may be required either to stay much longer in the sanctuary and perhaps work at a useful job inside or to enter into negotiations with the district attorney.

Some district attorneys may already have the right attitude and state of mind to carry out this new mode of justice, but some may need to be retrained. A new generation of attorneys may arise to actualize tsedeka in their work. They will hold the office of pretor, not of public prosecutor.

## Safe Conduct

A safe conduct is a document granted by a competent authority
that conveys immunity from arrest, either civil or prosecutive. It
gives a fugitive the right to travel to a place of sanctuary without
risking arrest on the way. In the past, safe conduct was, for obvious reasons, a necessary complement of the right of sanctuary.
It was an act of sovereignty, by which a sovereign visualized his
imposed peace. Documents of safe conduct were still in use during the eighteenth century. In Holland, as we have seen, the
princes of Orange granted them to persons seeking refuge in sanctuary towns.

Violations of safe conduct were rare. One known instance came
after the emperor Sigismund granted safe conduct to John Huss
to return home after he went to the Council of Constanz to justify himself against an indictment of heresy. In spite of the safe
conduct he was burned at the stake. A safe conduct granted to
Martin Luther after he was placed under imperial ban was respected.

Safe conduct will again be necessary for the proper functioning
of new sanctuaries. Fugitives from the law will be entitled to receive a document that guarantees security on their way to places
of sanctuary where they want to try to solve their conflicts. However, they will need to apply for safe conduct from the proper
authority.

Safe conduct might be of greatest value to those prosecutees
who are eager to apply for the eunomic system of crime control
but have already fallen into the hands of the administrators of
repressive justice. Special legal arrangements must be enacted in
order to grant any prisoner on remand the right to apply for safe
conduct. If the request is refused by the district attorney, the prisoner should be allowed to appeal to a court.

### Statutes of Sanctuary

Every place of sanctuary will be established and regulated by
law. Statutes will include rules regulating the jurisdiction and administration of the sanctuary, its external relations, and its competencies.

## Countering Objections

*Objection*: A sanctuary may in no time develop into a new kind of prison.

The argument is invalid. Prison inmates are not there by free will; they cannot escape except by committing another illegal act. They have entirely lost their identity. They suffer the daily humiliation of loss of human rights, lack of trust and self-respect, and exposure to possible violent acts of other inmates.

The residents in a sanctuary, on the other hand, are not in a place of confinement; they can leave at any moment they wish. They do not lose their human rights, are not debased by the extreme power of prosecution officers and guards, are able to surround themselves with those they love and trust, and are not exposed to violence. They are able to watch over their own conflict and keep their own situation in their own hands. Their responsible behavior is evoked, not their dishonesty. They remain full and complete human beings. While it is true that if a prosecuting authority is keen on apprehending them, their freedom of departure may be an illusion, but such departure can always be prepared by negotiation. As a matter of course, no sanctuary should ever allow a government-appointed warden to be its boss, as that might be the first step toward an eventual prison structure.

*Objection*: A sanctuary may soon develop into a new kind of ghetto.

In view of the ever-shifting population of a sanctuary, this is doubtful. In history the inhabitants of ghettos were forced to live there for life, but the residents of a modern sanctuary are expected to leave as soon as their dispute has been settled.

*Objection*: A sanctuary may develop into a place from which to launch violent acts of terrorism, raids, and assaults.

The argument is not fair. A modern prison serves this purpose much more than a sanctuary would. No maximum security prison in the world has ever been so tight as to make contacts between inmates and the outside world utterly impossible. The German

Baader Meinhoff terrorist group confined in Germany's maximum
security prison participated successfully in the preparation of terrorist activity in the world outside, and similar feats have occurred
in other countries.

In a sanctuary the chances are smaller because other residents
have more opportunities to observe what is going on. And if the
sanctuary statutes include a clause forbidding the preparation of
new crimes, the abusers could be thrown out and end up in
prison.

*Objection*: A sanctuary may in no time develop into a Mafialike
institution and develop a code of silence vis-à-vis civil authorities.

This possibility is real. It would, however, constitute an unfair
development of conflict resolution and thus induce the pretor to
withdraw the case from dispute settlement and commit it to the
repressive system of crime control. Any abuse of the eunomic
system will definitely lead to repressive control. Eunomie needs
fairness.

*Objection*: A sanctuary is an ancient institution improper for the
present time.

I have discussed this argument already, and it is invalid. Internal asylum is not an institution alien to our legal system. And
nobody would ever assume that a modern sanctuary would be
operated in the way sanctuaries operated several centuries ago.
Times change, and so do sanctuaries. But the concept of sanctuary does not contravene our legal system and has therefore the
right to exist.

# 6

# STRATEGIES OF CHANGE

How do we convince people and opinion makers that society and security would benefit from a change in the crime-control system toward an assensus-based model? What are to be the plans and means to accomplish a gradual change? Can we draft some plan of action or policy?

In this book I have, generally speaking, dealt only with the crime-control system of the Western world, its history and present development. Some sensitizing concepts also have been derived from Western culture, Jewish and Christian. Though comparisons have been made with other past and present cultures, the focus has always been on the Western system at large. That is possible because, in spite of differences and variations in intensity, the basic philosophy and presuppositions concerning crime control in North America and Western Europe are largely the same. How identical they are becomes immediately clear if we compare the Western system to that of Japan, a country having the same level of economic and industrial development but an entirely different cultural tradition. Japan has much less criminality and fewer prisoners, but that is due to a system of social control so fundamentally different from ours that it would be impossible to copy it.

Many people would agree that the present system of crime control is ineffective, unjust, unnecessarily cruel, and perhaps even counterproductive. But when it comes to the crunch, they hesitate, using such arguments as this one: Lots of people get terror-struck when they hear someone doubting the effectiveness of punitive criminal justice, let alone urging its abolition. As long as these fears exist, any reform of the system will meet the strongest resistance and make it impracticable.

Public fears are often seized on as a pretext to avoid taking a stand or to hamper a discussion of the crime-control system. Our first task is to examine these well-known public fears. They are real and should not be explained away. We must avoid the gross error made by many progressive or radical criminologists who do not take these complaints seriously. People want to be protected, and they are right to feel that way. A strategy of change therefore should not only include propositions concerning the prevention of crime but also make convincing arguments that an assensus-based system, if included in an effective prevention program, would eventually guarantee more protection and control than the repressive model.

## Public Fears

It has become a criminological cliché to hold the media responsible for arousing public fears and keeping them aroused. Elaborate, high-flown, and overdetailed coverage of violent crimes frightens many people. It makes them afraid to walk in our big cities and causes the wealthy to take costly precautions to protect their houses against burglary. In the United States it fuels the argument for the possession of arms.

It will be difficult to change the methods of the media. After all, people crave drama of all kinds. I prefer to point to another possible source of public fears. It may well be that progressive criminologists in the past century unintentionally have contributed to public fears. In too many progressive criminological enunciations, implicit excusing of the criminal can be found.

The first progressive statements, at the beginning of the twentieth century, were of a socialist nature. The unjust structure of capitalist society was blamed for criminality: change the socio-economic structure of society and criminality, which is just a bourgeois phenomenon, will vanish for the greater part. The few criminals still left are sick and should be treated in a psychiatric hospital. But society did not change in the way the early progressive criminologists had hoped it would. The powerful themselves became the greatest criminals and knew perfectly well how to use repressive crime control to get rid of their enemies. Still, the idea that criminals were not really responsible for their actions lived on in public opinion. When evildoers are no longer held responsible, the public gets frightened, and rightly so.

The next progressive movement was the so-called medical model. No longer were the structures of society to be blamed in the first place but the poor and miserable circumstances of early youth. The poor creatures are in need of treatment, not punishment. What the public understood of criminologists and psychotherapists was that in going even further in excusing the criminals, imagination was running away with them.

A later generation of radical criminologists during the 1970s even advocated "radical nonintervention." The less we interfere in the problem of criminality, it was alleged, the sooner we will reach a solution. When the public heard that, they thought the criminologists had gone crazy.

The so-called labeling school of progressive criminology made a good step in the right direction, but one step only. These criminologists put the focus of scientific attention not so much on the quarry as on the hunters. For the first time the reality of repression became a focus of interest. The contention that we are sending the wrong people to prison became a hot issue. But real public concerns again were being ignored. What good would it do to send all the wicked powerful to prison and let the common criminals stay outside? That is how the public understood it. The labeling school at large still ignored the real problem: the conflict between offender and victim, defendant and plaintiff. So the public once again felt deserted by the academics—and even more fearful of crimes.

Criminologists now began to show an increasing interest in the victims of crime. At last some attention was being given to their problems. But care for the victims is not sufficient if we do not solve the real problem: the conflict between offender and victim.

And who was the laughing third party behind all these flaws and foibles of criminology? The advocates and operators of the repressive system. Just by referring to the "irresponsible" statements of progressive criminologists they cleared the road for more and more repression. They gave a distinct and unclouded promise to the public: we will arrest all the evildoers, put them away, and thereby protect you and the rest of society. These are false promises, of course, but people often tend to believe in the easiest solution offered. We see the result: an increase in both the prison population and criminality.

No proposition to change the crime-control system will ever be successful if the justified fears of the public are not taken seriously. That is why I stress that a eunomic system is not soft; it does not excuse criminals but makes them responsible.

## Prevention

Reform of the crime-control system must include an effective strategy for crime prevention and social control. Many large cities in the past few decades have, in a careless and inexcusable way, neglected preventive social control. Now, finally coming to our senses and becoming aware of the collapse of preventive social control, we often can think of no better solution than increasing repressive control, usually with counterproductive effects.

Take the case of public transport. We once had ticket sellers or ticket collectors on every streetcar or train. Garages and public parking facilities too usually had ticket sellers. Though we may not have been aware of it at the time, these people did much more than sell or collect tickets. They embodied social control; many even wore uniforms. Then, to economize on salaries, ticket collectors were replaced by stamping machines and other devices. After a while the number of fare dodgers increased by up to 40 percent. Vandalism increased spectacularly, so much that every few years the furniture in streetcars and trains has to be renewed. But worst of all, violence in public transport increased dramatically. However, decision makers in public transport failed to rise to the occasion. Instead of rescinding their actions and reintroducing preventive control by ticket sellers and collectors, they often preferred to increase repressive control by introducing cop patrols. The result, as could be expected, was increased violence against the controllers as well as the public.

## Drugs

Administrators of repressive justice are using the drug problem as a justification for harsher punitive activity and for new prison construction. Given the huge increase in drug-related crime, they say, we need more prisons. The argument serves them well. For in the past thirty years criticism of the repressive system has been increasing, and the administrators of repressive justice were afraid they were losing ground. But now look! There is a new justification: we need new prisons to control the drug problem by incarcerating all those drug users, traffickers, pushers, dealers, junkies, growers, and peddlers.

Even reasonable people who acknowledge that the repressive system may be no good will argue that we must fight against illegal drugs and drug abuse, one of the greatest evils threatening our society. So, they say, let's postpone changing the crime-control system for a while, until better days are here again.

Because of the seriousness of the problem and in order to find its roots and put it in the right perspective, let's start with a short historical survey. Globally speaking, one can distinguish cultures in two groups: those that tolerate alcohol and those that tolerate other kinds of mind-altering drugs. Cultures tolerating both are rare.

The ancient Greeks had their highly beloved god of wine, Dionysus, whom they usually represented under the influence of his favorite beverage. But the adepts of the Greek mystery cults who used hallucinogenic drugs were often persecuted, even massacred.

Native Americans knew and used natural hallucinogens for centuries, also for religious rites. But they were ravaged when European invaders gave them alcohol, which their bodies could not tolerate.

In the European Middle Ages, alcohol was not supposed to create problems. It was even sacred, for wine was used in the Eucharist. The wine cellars of most monasteries were well stocked, and monks engaged in wine making, brewery, and liquor distilling.

Problems arose at the time of the witch hunts. It was generally believed that so-called witches used hallucinogenic drugs, and many probably did. The great witch hunts between 1470 and 1600 can easily be explained as a war against these drugs. But medieval monks too grew cannabis and other hallucinogenic plants in their herb gardens. It is not surprising that there were so many mystics in those days: they knew quite well how to reach "ecstasy." But the European culture apparently had difficulty in tolerating two types of stimulants.

Between 1600 and 1900 drugs apparently were not experienced as a government problem. In the nineteenth century opium could be found in most kitchens of Europe, used as a pain killer. In the days before aspirin and modern dentistry, it was considered a godsend, given even to babies. Not being a forbidden fruit, it created few problems. Abuse was marginal.

In truth, the Western colonial powers profited greatly from the trade in opium. The colonial government of the Netherlands East Indies made the trade a government monopoly, and this continued until 1941. The British government did likewise in India, and when the Chinese government wanted to stop importation of English opium, Britain declared war on China so that English profits could be assured. That was not a war against drugs but a war in favor of drugs.

So why has the twentieth century seen a revival of the struggle against drugs similar to the medieval witch hunts? For one thing, opium was no longer needed as a pain killer after aspirin was invented in the late nineteenth century. But that cannot be the only reason.

When other drugs were still hardly a problem, alcohol was. So Americans made the problem worse in the late 1920s by using the wrong tool: repression. The horrendous result is well known: a black market in alcohol trade resulting in widespread gangsterism. In the early thirties Americans acknowledged their mistake but the calamity had already happened. The gangsters who had grown fat had to look for new business, and they found it in arms and drugs. Drugs were made a problem not by the few drug users but by racketeers with their obscure influence on the rulers of the country. Rather foolishly—or perhaps for their own profit—successive administrations ran into the trap set for them and created a new forbidden fruit.

After the Second World War the Western European countries had no worse drug problems than they had ever had. But the powerful United States government urged all these countries to introduce antidrug legislation and thus to create forbidden fruits—exactly what the gangsters needed. As could have been foreseen, the forbidden fruit complex resulted in a huge black market in drugs and steadily rising prices.

Have the drug gangsters infiltrated Western governments? In view of the zillions of dollars in profit that can be made, it is, from a statistical point of view, impossible that all of the many thousands of civil servants in charge of the war on drugs in North America and Western Europe have remained honest. There is no conclusive evidence so far that high government officials have been involved, but it certainly is evident that every step-up in the antidrug war has increased drug profits and worked in the interests of the international drug trade.

Is there a way out? Unfortunately, there is only one way out, and that is back to legalization, a logical step so frowned upon by government officials. Of course, few persons would favor the immediate legal sale of either "soft" or "hard" drugs. The situation has deteriorated so much, owing to the foolishness of our governments, that change will take time. It will be difficult for the rulers just to admit they were wrong.

But legalization will be easy, compared with our present repressive methods. If drugs are made available to addicts in government-controlled clinics, dispensaries, and wards, these people will have no need to commit crimes to get drugs. Fewer users will become addicts. Far fewer young children will be hooked. Prices on the black markets will drop sharply. When profits drop, fewer dealers will be interested in pushing sales. The gangsters will look for a different source of income, and the farmers will go back to growing coffee. Within a few years the problem will have greatly diminished, and the authorities will have lost their argument against making changes in the crime-control system.

## Public Cooperation

What kind of people would be inclined to cooperate in the start of a eunomic system of crime control and be willing to settle their disputes this way?

An individual's disposition to settle disputes, as research in this field has shown, is closely related to his or her level of education. Persons with more education tend to be better able to express their thoughts, to discuss their problems, and to have a greater expectation of outwitting their opponents by their own skills or by the skills of experts they can hire. They learn to control their emotions and replace them by rational considerations. As a result, they are less afraid than others to enter upon dispute settlement, believing that they have a good chance of reaching an agreement favorable to them.

The shrewd skills of the better educated and their expert helpers might be raised as an important argument against the introduction of a eunomic system: the socially unskilled would always get the short end of the stick. But this abuse can be avoided if the unskilled always have the opportunity to join forces. Less-educated people faced with difficult social problems tend to turn to collective action. A lower level of education does not lead people to dislike dispute settlement but rather to prefer to act within a group.

At any rate, most dispute settlements will as a rule be successful only if worked out in groups. Not only the wrong doers but also victims will find greater satisfaction by working in groups. It will be the pretor's task to protect the less powerful and less educated against abuses by the more powerful and better educated.

## Education

As Raymond Shonholtz observed, "People in modern society have been deskilled to solve their own conflicts. They have to be reskilled." Shonholtz opened a school program in San Francisco to teach children that when they have problems they should not run at once to higher authorities and ask for help. They should rather sit down and palaver together to find solutions. Shonholtz also convened Saturday training courses in conflict management for people in neighborhoods.

With respect to the development of sound methods of crime conflict resolution, the professional overemphasis on individual casework has been a great setback. The practice of social workers should rather be in the direction of conflict casework. The conflict, not the person, is the case, and both offender and victim, defendant and plaintiff, are the clients. Social studies curricula should put dispute settlement of crime conflicts in the forefront of training policy. If a eunomic system gets a chance to develop in the near future, its flourishing will depend in large measure on social workers well trained in facilitating and mediating crime conflicts. As long as people have not yet been well "reskilled," they will need social workers to guide and counsel them.

The big risk here is the disreputable phenomenon of professionalization. Social workers have not always understood that education is in principle an endeavor to make the educator superfluous. Nobody wants social workers to move into the power position now held by repressive controllers. That would be a fundamental error, comparable to what happened with the medical model, when psychiatrists tried to preempt legal judgment.

It should not be forgotten that dispute settlement in itself may have an educational effect. By settling their disputes and contributing to the resolution of their conflicts, people—offenders and victims—learn how to behave like good citizens.

## Opinion Makers

Opinion makers represent an intangible category. Nobody has appointed them; they have no titles. And yet anyone who raises a novel issue must take the opinion makers into account. They can wreck an initiative or save it.

Who are they? Of course, members of the media pretend to play first fiddle among opinion makers on almost every issue of social importance or social triviality. But every social issue has its particular category of opinion makers. In the field of crime con-

trol they are lawyers, not only practicing lawyers but also those
teaching at law schools.

## Media

The role of the media has been one of the most discussed topics in criminology—and to little avail. We are still as wise or as
ignorant as we ever were on this matter. It has never been proved
that people commit crimes because they watch violence on televi-
sion. At most, TV programs may teach them some new methods.

It is true that in violence-prone countries one sees lots of violence on TV and a press crammed with violence in full detail. The
United States in particular has a reputation in this regard. But it
does not follow that media coverage provokes violence. It would
of course be better if violent movies were more honest. Violent
screen heroes who display their courage in man-to-man fights
should not then be shown dusting off their clothes unhurt, but
should rather be shown the next morning in the hospital with a
brain hemorrhage. And children should not watch every cartoon
tomcat comfortably surviving an exploding bomb. Making certain
that heroes of violent TV movies invariably end up in a hospital
might be of some help. But it is doubtful that it would substantially reduce violence in society.

Violent TV shows are a mirror or outcome rather than a cause
of violent tendencies in society. One might even argue that violence on TV has a cathartic effect on watchers. If so, there might
even be more violence in society without violent TV shows and
movies. We will never know.

It would make more sense, seen in the perspectives of this
book, if some really good filmmakers or TV producers turned
their attention away from their customary unreal and boring
themes to dispute-settlement themes in which the goodies outwit
the baddies. Police films have given it a try in recent years, but it
might be a good idea if a Society for the Promotion of Eunomic
Crime Control (see the last section of this chapter) would present
an award for the best movie or TV series on crime conflict resolution. Such a national society could also bring media directors
and journalists together to discuss a self-imposed code for the representation of violence. If, as some believe, a great part of human

conduct is imitative behavior, people might as well imitate crime conflict resolution.

## The Legal Profession

With regard to changes in the crime-control system, legal professionals and law schools are the opinion makers par excellence. Without their cooperation, any reform program in the field of crime control is doomed to fail. I include in this group not only private attorneys but also prosecuting attorneys, judges, and many legislators.

It is remarkable how far the "noble office" with regard to criminal law has deviated from its illustrious predecessors in Roman antiquity. Nonetheless, we are fortunate that with regard to civil law and most other parts of the legal system, the legal profession remains intact. The profession has deteriorated chiefly in crime control. As already noted, our present system of crime control does not deserve the name of law. Lawyers themselves should protest against it. By urging other legal professionals to become aware of the ancient traditions of their profession and to claim again the noble skills of conflict resolution and dispute settlement in cases of crime without unnecessary interference by a prosecuting agency, lawyers can be of great help, both in doing the right work and in promoting the right idea of crime control.

However, a catch may lie in wait. Legal structures vary enormously from country to country. In Europe litigation proneness has not reached the level it has in North America. The legal system in the United States, for example, allows and promotes much litigation, a tendency absent in Europe. Europeans apparently get their due more often without appealing to the judiciary. The relative number of lawyers is many times larger in the United States than in Europe. But the matter of peculiarities of various legal structures goes far beyond the scope of this book.

Better training of young lawyers, with research into the problems of crime dispute settlement, is the province of law schools, faculties of law, and inns of court. For many law students, criminal law is their least favorite subject. Here they must do without the typical jurisprudence of finding a resolution to a conflict in accordance with law. The present criminal law curriculum is not training in jurisprudent skills but brainwashing. Students are urged to accept uncritically the crazy development of our crime-control system.

A few law schools in some countries, it is true, include courses of training and research in conflict resolution. However, the total number of courses in crime dispute settlement can be counted on the fingers of two hands. And only recently have some universities set up courses in which students are taught greater social aware-ness in the application of legal skills to resolve crime conflicts.

The least our law schools should do is to make students more critical of the repressive system. Their courses should make stu-dents aware of the possibilities lawyers would have if they were allowed to apply their civil law skills within a nonrepressive crimi-nal law system. That too may be a point of action for a Society for the Promotion of Eunomic Crime Control. Such a society could promote the establishment of special chairs in crime conflict resolution and the implementation of research programs.

*Police*

A better system of crime control cannot be successful without the collaboration of the police. But again and again police will need to be reminded of their essential task: the prevention and resolution of conflicts. This task must occupy first place in police instructions. Police unfortunately have tolerated or even relished their military image as fighters against criminals, courageous sol-diers against state enemies. But police themselves have been vic-timized by the repressive system that divides society into goodies and baddies.

One solution might be to split the police force in conformity with a dual system of crime control, one part of the force sus-taining the eunomic system of crime control and the other part (perhaps with different uniforms and badges) supporting the re-pressive system. Such a dual force need not be internally antago-nistic. Each part would support the other in the implementation of their tasks, handing over cases to one another. But the restruc-turing of police forces goes beyond the scope of this book.

## *Religious Leaders*

The influence of religion and religious leaders varies enormously from country to country. As we have seen, crime in the religious mind often is burdened with guilt feelings. To get rid of them, religious leaders often repress the topic of crime control. Still, the influence of religious leaders may permeate a nation, and it must be examined.

We have noted that many churches suddenly became active in allowing their premises to be used as sanctuaries for persons who were politically persecuted. Why not activate churches to redress the damage Christianity brought to the crime-control system by utterly wrong interpretations of Bible texts and by creating vicious institutions such as the Inquisition, godparent of our repressive system? Both Protestants and Catholics now have a chance to do penitence by initiating new ways of crime control.

Among Jews there has always been an interest in tsedeka. Some of their religious leaders have understood its message in relation to modern law. Let us hope that Judaism will again contribute to the improvement and radical change of the crime-control system.

## Citizens' Initiatives

Dissatisfaction with the repressive system is far from new. Many citizens have taken initiatives to improve the situation. Usually they have attempted to help ex-prisoners with probation and aftercare services. But the development of the welfare state, both in Europe and America, has resulted in co-optation of many ancient aftercare initiatives, bringing them in line with the aims of the repressive system.

In the early 1980s we witnessed a new initiative, the founding in Toronto of the International Conference on Penal Abolition. It has held several international meetings, in Warsaw, Amsterdam, Montreal, and Bloomington, Indiana. Early meetings focused attention just on prison abolition. But use of the term *abolition* strikes terror in members of the public, who interpret it as some kind of harebrained utopian scheme that would make all of us defenseless against violent criminals. Any citizen's initiative, to be fruitful, must stress not so much that something is to be abolished but that something is to be established.

Another obstacle facing international associations is the difference in legal structure of partaking nations. There should be not one international group but a national association in each country that can adapt propositions in accord with its particular legal structure. It might be called the National Society for the Promotion of Eunomic Crime Control or the National Association for Tsedeka Justice. The latter name would suit any church-oriented initiative for the improvement of crime control. A society by that name has already been founded in Calgary.

These societies might take any of several possible initiatives: special chairs for crime conflict resolution at law schools, schools of social work, and police academies; new research programs in crime conflict resolution; awards for meritorious movie and TV productions or instances of conflict resolution; experimental sanctuaries; and political action to convince legislators to add a paragraph to the law of criminal procedure stating that if the two parties in a crime conflict have established a reasonable and fair agreement for the resolution of their dispute, public prosecution renounces its right of further indictment.

Some people might call the ideas in this book utopian. They would be wrong, because these ideas are based on sound legal principle: conflict resolution. And anyway, such critics forget that many utopian proposals have become reality. They should read or reread the work of Thomas More, who coined the word *Utopia*. They will see that quite a few of his proposals have come true.

# CONCLUSIONS

B ECAUSE THE PRESENT system of crime control results in anomic situations in society, we must institute next to it a eunomic system of crime control allowing for active responsibilities of
those concerned. In a eunomic system of control, crime is no
longer defined as a conflict between criminal and society but
rather between accused and victim/plaintiff.

A eunomic system is based on the necessity of crime conflict
resolution by dispute settlement. Plaintiff and accused would have
a constitutional and inalienable right to demand that their conflict
be resolved by negotiation instead of punishment. The state prosecution would no longer have the monopoly of crime control if a
better solution can be found. Any system of crime control should,
as a consequence, offer participants, both the offender/defendant
and the victim/plaintiff, a dual choice: the present repressive system of punishment or a eunomic system of conflict resolution.
The actual criminal procedure must acknowledge the right of the
victim/plaintiff to intervene in the procedure at any time and demand that it be concluded with conflict resolution instead of punishment. To the law of criminal procedure a new basic paragraph
must be added, reading as follows: If the two parties in a crime
conflict have established a reasonable and fair agreement on the
resolution of their conflict, the public prosecution renounces its
right of further indictment.

To facilitate conflict resolution in cases of violent crime, the
state must allow the foundation and maintenance of locations of
sanctuary in several regions of the country. The law would provide the rules for such institutions. So-called alternative kinds of
punishment, such as community work, constitute a great danger
for fair justice and legal morality as long as they are embedded in
a repressive system of punishment. They should be allowed only

if based on fair legislation providing legal protection of participants. Finally, a new state function must be established by law:
that of pretorship. The pretor would be in charge of surveying
the course of crime conflict resolution and dispute settlement,
with the duty to intervene if the eunomic system is abused.

# NOTES

## 1. The Idea of Justice

1. The works of Martin Buber, the Jewish-German philosopher (1878–1965) has been a prime inspiration for this book. Buber was a great innovator in Biblical translation. Older translations into European languages, such as the English Jacobean version and the Dutch state translation of 1639, may have expanded the languages, but they were often inadvertently or intentionally wrong. Buber, in his translation of Tenach (the Old Testament) into German, avoided mistakes by creating new words in order to come as near as possible to the original meanings.

2. Some of my remarks concerning justice reveal the influence of Julius Stone. In *Human Law and Human Justice*, Stone has rightly observed the tensions between justice and law (pp. 9–34) and the law of nature (pp. 36–81). But despite his knowledge of Biblical concepts, he has failed to understand the notion of tsedeka.

3. See Stone, pp. 306–10.

4. Aristotle almost never links his discussion of justice to the concept of punishment, and when he does it involves the punishment of slaves. Perhaps he thought that punishment did not belong to the domain of justice, except in regard to slaves. In any case, Aristotle's example lends support to the view that the Greek notion of law by and large excluded punishment. See Aristotle, *Topica* 12. Plato argued it did, but there again we have to realize the double meaning of the Greek word *poinē*.

5. See Stone, pp. 14–18. Similarly, Jacques Ellul, p. 22: when there is no longer an idea of the notion of justice in law there will be no longer a normative factor in legal practice. In that case law is only serving the concern for immediate social utility and not for justice.

6. Ovid, *Epistulae ex Ponto*, IV.

7. See H. Butterfield, *The Whig Interpretation of History*, London, 1931; and D. J. Boorstin, "The Humane Study of Law," *Yale Law Journal* 57 (1948), and "Tradition and Method in Legal History," *Harvard Law Review* 54 (1941).

8. For detailed discussions on avoiding revenge and punishment in ancient and other cultures, see C. F. Bayerschmidt and L. M. Hollander, *Njáls Saga*, New York, 1955; Viola Garfield, *Tsimshian Clan and Society*, Washington, D.C., 1939; V. Aubert, "Competition and Dissensus: Two Types of Conflict and Conflict Resolution," *Journal of Conflict Resolution* 7 (1963); and J. Galtung, "Institutionalized Conflict Resolution," *Journal of Peace Research* (1965).

9. The answer to the pivotal question of whether the Romans ever had punitive law lies in the fact that they never had a public prosecutor. We can

infer this fact from the Lex Valeria de Provocatione (about B.C. 300), which strictly limited the power of any magistrate with regard to punishment. Only with the rule of the Christian emperor Theodosius (401–50) do we see a beginning of *cognitio extra ordinem*, which appears to prefigure the later Roman Catholic Inquisition. The term *extra ordinary procedure* got a sinister reputation in later punitive law, as it allowed torture. The ordinary procedure was, like Roman law, bent on assessment of damage. See V. Arangio-Ruiz et al., pp. 251–53, and B. Santalucia, pp. 138ff. According to W. Kunkel, p. 16, the procedures of "penal" Roman law served only the determination of the guilt of the accused and never the implication of any punishment in the modern sense. Vis-à-vis the accused, one finds exclusively a plaintiff and never a public magistrate, for, except in political cases, there has never been such a magistrate. It always remained an accusatorial procedure—not, as in English trials, between public prosecution and accused but between plaintiff and accused. Assuming some kind of monopolized public prosecution in ordinary criminal cases is an anachronism of the worst kind. The praetor was really the key figure in the procedural games of Roman law. As president of the *quaestiones perpetuae*, the praetor could decide whether a case should follow public or private legal lines. It is only under the *domitiat* after Diocletian that some kind of punitive prosecution on behalf of the imperial state can be noticed, but it never became a state monopoly. See also B. Nicholas, pp. 208ff., who points out that the Romans never distinguished between crime in a public sense and crime in a private sense.

10. The mysterious origin in our culture of punishment, in the sense of intentional infliction of suffering on an accused, with simultaneous omission of duty to repair and liberation from guilt, has been studied by many scholars astonished by the existence of such a barbaric and antisocial phenomenon. The German historian Hans Fehr called it one of the great problems of history. We know there was a long epoch in which punishment did not exist and one day it was suddenly there, says V. Achter, p. 10. Light is thrown on the question by P. W. A. Immink, pp. 33ff., who shows that the origin of the notion of punishment can be found in the Roman institution of slavery, in particular in the Leges Barbarorum. A freeman could always buy himself out of vengeance and offer repair or redress, but a slave, who did not have free disposition of his physical labor, could never redeem himself. He had no choice but to submit to physical punishment and suffering. This system, together with the Inquisition, served as a model of punitive criminal law. An echo of the slave origin of punishment can be found in the mean-spirited expression in the Fourteenth Amendment to the United States Constitution: "all servitude is abolished except penal servitude."

11. Cf. J. Guiraud, pp. 208–10: to avoid an obtrusion of the Inquisition into the south of France that might have meant a reduction of royal power, Philippe le Bel adopted some inquisitory penal measures. In other words, the wolves taught him how to whine.

12. The only other culture that developed a repressive system of punishment seems to be China in the early stages of its development. China was

perhaps the first culture in world history to form a state in the modern sense of the word, i.e., an organization with civil servants salaried by a central administration; see Herrlee G. Creel, *The Origins of Statecraft in China*, Chicago, 1970. This parallel case may confirm our conclusion that state formation is important to the origin of a system of punishment.

13. The concept of tsedeka has been discussed by a number of scholars. See, for example, J. Pedersen, pp. 336–411; R. Mach, pp. 1–51; K. H. Fahlgren, passim; N. H. Snaith, pp. 51–79; and E. R. Achtermeier, passim.

14. Luther's doctrine of the two realms and the two regiments has given rise to an abundant literature. See W. D. J. Cargill Thompson, *The Political Thought of Martin Luther*, Totowa, N.J., 1984, pp. 36–62; F. Edward Cranz, *An Essay on the Development of Luther's Thought on Justice, Law and Society*, Cambridge, Mass., 1959; and Gérard Mairet, "Le Protestantisme et la justification du glaive," in F. Châtelet.

15. Martin Buber, in the preamble to his highly reliable German translation of the Bible, gives a detailed account of the terms he chose for the notion of tsedeka justice. He did not use the general German word for "justice" (*Gerechtigkeit*) because by using that word he might have introduced the entire burden of misunderstandings that go with the Latin word. He found or coined other words, such as *Bewährung* (genuineness and substantiation), *Bewahrheitung* (confirmation of truth), and *Befreiung* (liberation and release of guilt). Perhaps one day a similar translation genius will arise in the English-speaking world. I humbly offer these words of advice to anyone really interested in studying Biblical messages: beware of all translations! Learn Hebrew, and if you are unwilling or unable, hands off! Too much harm has already been done by the abuse of Biblical texts through wrong interpretation and faulty or abominable translation.

16. The concept of truth in the Bible, compared with the Greek tradition in Western culture, has been well expressed by Boman, p. 200: "The Greek scholars have been searching for the objective truth of that which is, clarity and evidence. Hebrew thought by contrast searched for the certainty of the truth of life, history, and morale. Greek thought is architectonic; Biblical thought is essential. It is of course a dualism that has permeated our Western philosophy ever since." The two courses of thought have been creating and denouncing one another for centuries; the "truth" is that they need one another; they constitute the two legs of Western thought and culture. The most outstanding Christian philosophers, such as Augustine and Thomas Aquinas, have been aware of this notion of truth. However, they did not propose it as essential but rather as a sometimes necessary deviation. As Thomas says, "Licet veritatem occultare prudenter sub alique dissimulatione" (*Summa Theologica* 110, 3 and 4); cf. G. Del Vecchio, pp. 179–84. Sartre understood it quite well in his famous remarks concerning "Mauvaise Foi" (*L'Etre et le néant*, passim). The repressive system of crime control promises convicts reintegration into society while making them suffer pain—and while knowing full well that reintegration will never follow: that is indeed bad faith. But what else can one expect from a repressive system?

17. For details on Biblical notions of retaliation, see D. Daube, pp. 102–54.

18. Maimonides, Mishne Torah, Sepher Shoftim, Hilchot Sanhedrin, XVII,7. In *The Code of Maimonides*, bk. 14, "The Book of Judges," trans. A. Hershman, New Haven, Conn., 1949.

19. Ideas in this section have been greatly influenced by the thought of Kierkegaard. He treated the concepts everywhere in his work. Sartre (*Le sequestré d'Altona*) and Camus (*Caligula* and *La chute*) followed in Kierkegaard's footsteps, stressing the uneasiness of a generation that feels guilty but does not know how to relieve itself. A punitive legal system such as ours, incessantly stressing the reality of guilt without offering a possiblity of relief, is really the greatest cruelty imaginable. One of the best studies of guilt and culpability is John McKenzie, *Guilt: Its Meaning and Significance*.

20. Ideas in this section have been influenced by Henri Bergson's *Essai sur les données immédiates de la conscience* (1889), in which he refers to procession, inversion, and conversion.

## 2. Two Concepts of Law

1. The Biblical notion of Torah has, like tsedeka, suffered misunderstandings. It has also been the subject of many studies. See, e.g., J. Pedersen, pp. 292ff, 571 and 657; Martin Buber's works; and Buber's introduction to his Bible translation in Buber and Rosenzweig. On ancient Jewish concepts, see Max Kadushin, *The Rabbinic Mind*, New York, 1952; Solomon Schechter, *Aspects of Rabbinic Theology* and *Major Concepts of the Talmud*, New York, 1909 and 1961; Carol Klein, *The Credo of Maimonides*, New York, 1958; and George Foot Moore, *Judaism*, Cambridge, England, 1927. On Jewish law, see George Horowitz, *The Spirit of Jewish Law*, New York, 1963; Anthony Phillips, *Ancient Israel's Criminal Law*, Oxford, 1970; and Mayer Sulzberger, *Ancient Hebrew Law of Homicide*, Philadelphia, 1915.

2. The concept of eunomie is very old, but it is new to the social sciences, more or less this author's invention. I cannot therefore refer the reader to other writings on the subject.

3. The terms *criminalize* and *criminalization* are comparatively new, dating from the end of the 1960s. In some languages the term *crime* was already in legal usage to denote that a particular act is seen as a "crime" (felony) and not a misdemeanor.

4. The phenomenon of stigmatization is too often overlooked in legal studies on criminal law. Conventional theorists dislike the concept because it does not fit into their neat justificatory theories on punishment and might give them a bad conscience. In the social sciences, though, it has received much attention. The works of E. Goffman have become classic. See also H. Bianchi and U. E. Gerhardt and M. E. J. Wadsworth.

## 3. The Assensus Model

1. Many social scientists agree that consensus is utopian if not fraud; see A. Etzioni, *Complex Organizations*, pp. 127–151. Societal energy, says Etzioni,

makes place for the uncertainties of consensus and the limitations set on established powers by contesting powers. In short, internal dynamics functions.

2. One of the great theoreticians of dissensus has been Dahrendorf. He speaks of conflict where I would prefer the term *dissensus*, for dissensus presupposes the ideology behind the conflict by which the contesting groups make themselves visible. The French sociologist Balandier uses the term *dissidence*. That is somewhat imprudent, because dissidence usually connotes religious dissent—or politcal dissent where politics has become religion.

## 4. Dispute Settlement

1. On Mennonite initiatives in North America, see R. Shonholtz "New Justice Theory and Practice," in H. Bianchi and R. V. Swaaningen, *Abolitionism: Proceedings of the Second International Congress on Abolitionism in Amsterdam, 1985*, pp. 228–238, and his contribution in R. V. Swaaningen et al., *A tort et a travers: Liber amicorum Herman Bianchi*.

## 5. Sanctuary

1. On sanctuaries in medieval England, see J. C. Cox.

2. On cities of sanctuary during this period in the Netherlands, see M. Gijswijt Hofstra. Unfortunately, this kind of research is still lacking for England, France, and other countries of the Western world. The situation in the United States regarding sanctuaries has been ignored by historians. There must have been some. As far as religious dissidents are concerned, American colonies were sanctuary to one another: Catholics in Maryland, Quakers in Pennsylvania, Puritans in Massachusetts. However, when the young United States started to develop, the glorious time of sanctuaries was over and the United States became even a champion of the new repressive punitive laws of the Enlightenment.

3. See G. McEoin, ed., and J. Scheffer, ed. Scheffer's book, approved by the World Alliance of Reformed Churches, discusses not only asylums at the present day but also their religious and political aspects. It also proposes the use of sanctuaries for prosecuted criminals.

# SELECTED BIBLIOGRAPHY

## Introduction

Appel, G. N., and T. N. Madan. *Choice and Morality in Anthropological Perspective: Essays in Honor of Derek Freeman*. Albany: SUNY Press, 1988.

Atkinson, A. *Social Order and the General Theory of Strategy*. London: Routledge & Kegan Paul, 1990.

Barnes, H. E. *Historical Sociology: Its Origins and Development*. New York: Philosophical Library, 1948.

Beauvoir, S. de. *Pour une morale de l'ambiguité*. Paris: Gallimard, 1947.

Bergson, H. *Essai sur les données immédiates de la conscience*. Paris: Librairie Félix Alcan, 1920.

———. *Les deux sources de la morale et de la religion*. Paris: Presses Universitaires de France, 1932.

Bianchi, H. *Position and Subject-Matter of Criminology*. Amsterdam: North Holland, 1956.

———. *Wij en de misdaad*. Amsterdam: Wereldbibliotheek, 1959.

———. *Ethiek van het straffen*. Nijkerk: Callenbach, 1964.

———. *Basismodellen in de criminologie*. Deventer: Kluwer, 1979.

———. "L'imagination prisonniere." In *La prison, le bagne et l'histoire*, ed. J. G. Petit. Geneva: Médicine et Hygiene. 1984.

———. *Vers un droit d'asile intieur, plaidoyer pour la réintroduction des asiles*. Vol. 7 in *Droit et cultures*. Paris: Editions de la Maison des Sciences, 1984.

———. *Politiek en criminaliteit*. Kampen: Kok, 1992.

Bianchi, H., and R. v. Swaaningen. *Abolitionism: Proceedings of the Second International Congress on Abolitionism in Amsterdam, 1985*. Amsterdam: Free University Press, 1986.

Cashet, T. [Herman Bianchi]. *A Breviary of Torment: Poetry on Torture*. San Francisco: GLB, 1991.

Chaunu, P. *Histoire et imagination: La transition*. Paris: Presses Universitaires de France, 1980.

Crook, R. H. *An Introduction to Christian Ethics*. Englewood Cliffs, N.J.: Prentice-Hall, 1990.

Diamond, M. L. *Martin Buber, Jewish Existentialist*. New York: Oxford University Press, 1960.

Diener, E., and R. Crandall. *Ethics in Social and Behavioral Research*. Chicago: University of Chicago Press, 1978.

Ezorsky, G. *Philosophical Perspectives on Punishment*. Albany: SUNY Press, 1972.

Fleming, M. *Of Crimes and Rights*. New York: Norton, 1978.

Gutiérrez, G. *A Theology of Liberation*. New York: Orbis Books, 1973.

Guyau, M. *Esquisse d'une morale sans obligation, ni sanction*. Paris: Félix Alcan, 1885.

Habermas, J. *Moral Consciousness and Communicative Action*. Trans. S. W. Nicholson. Cambridge: MIT Press, 1990.

Hagan, J. *Deterrence Reconsidered*. Beverly Hills: Sage, 1982.

———. *Structural Criminology*. Cambridge: Polity Press, 1988.

———. *Modern Criminology: Crime, Criminal Behavior and Its Control*. New York: McGraw-Hill, 1989.

Hart, H. L. A. *Punishment and Responsibility: Essays in the Philosophy of Law*. London: Oxford University Press, 1968.

McShea, R. J. *Morality and Human Nature: A New Route to Ethical Theory*. Philadelphia: Temple University Press, 1990.

Mapel, D. *Social Justice Reconsidered: The Problem of Appropriate Precision in a Theory of Justice*. Urbana: University of Illinois Press, 1989.

Martin, R. *Criminological Thought: Pioneers and Present*. New York: Macmillan, 1990.

Nagel, T. *Equality and Partiality*. New York: Oxford University Press, 1991.

Nerlich, G. *Values and Valuing: Speculations on the Ethical Life of Persons*. Oxford: Clarendon Press, 1989.

*New Directions in the Study of Justice, Law and Social Control*. Prepared by the School of Justice Studies, Arizona State University, Tempe. New York: Plenum Press, 1990.

Packer, H. L. *The Limits of Criminal Sanction*. Stanford: Stanford University Press, 1968.

Plack, A. *Plädoyer für die Abschaffung des Strafrechts*. Munich: List Verlag, 1974.

Primorac, I. *Justifying Legal Punishment*. Atlantic Highlands, N.J.: Humanities Press International, 1989.

Quinney, R. *The Social Reality of Crime*. Boston: Little, Brown, 1970.

Raphael, D. D. *Moral Judgement*. London: Allen & Unwin, 1955.

Rescher, N. *The Coherence Theory of Truth*. Oxford: Clarendon Press, 1973.

———. *Ethical Idealism*. Berkeley: University of California Press, 1987.

————. *Rationality: A Philosophical Inquiry into the Nature of and the Rationale of Reason.* Oxford: Clarendon Press, 1988.

Rex, J. *Sociology and the Demystification of the Modern World.* London: Routledge & Kegan Paul, 1974.

Shoham, S. *Society and the Absurd.* Oxford: Basil Blackwell, 1974.

Vivas, E. *The Moral Life and the Ethical Life.* Chicago: Regnery, 1963.

## 1. The Idea of Justice

Achter, V. *Die Geburt der Strafe.* Frankfurt on Main: Vittorio Klostermann, 1951.

Achtermeier, E. R. *The Gospel of Righteousness: A Study in the Meaning of Sdq and Its Derivatives in the Old Testament.* New York: Columbia University Press, 1959.

Arangio-Ruiz, V., A. Guarino, and G. Pugliese. *Il diritto romano.* Rome: Jouvence, 1984.

Badinter, R., ed. *Une autre justice: Etudes publiées sous la direction de Histoire de la Justice.* Paris: Fayard, 1989.

Barr, J. *The Semantics of Biblical Language.* Oxford: Oxford University Press, 1961.

Basaglia, F. and F. *Les criminels de la paix: Recherches sur les intellectuels et leurs techniques comme préposés à l'oppression.* Paris: Presses Universitaires de France, 1980.

Bevan, E. R., and C. Singer, eds. *The Legacy of Israel.* Oxford: Clarendon Press, 1927.

Boman, T. *Hebrew Thought Compared with Greek.* London: SCM Press, 1960.

Buber, M., and F. Rosenzweig. *Die Schrift und Ihre Verdeutschung.* Berlin: Schocken, 1936.

Burdese, A., ed. *Idee vecchie e nuove sul diritto criminale romano: Publicazioni della Facoltà di Giuriprudenza dell' Università de Padova.* Padua: Cedam, 1988.

Castaban, Y. *Magie et sorcellerie à l'epoque moderne.* Paris: Albin Michel, 1979.

Châtelet, F. *Histoire des idéologies.* 3 vols. Paris: Hachette, 1978.

Cohen, B. *Law and Tradition in Judaism.* New York: Jewish Theological Seminary of America, 1959.

Daube, D. *Studies in Biblical Law.* Cambridge: Cambridge University Press, 1947.

Delumeau, J. *Le péché et la peur: La culpabilisation en Occident.* Paris: Fayard, 1983.

Del Vecchio, G. *Philosophie du droit.* Paris: Dalloz, 1953.

―――. *La justice–la vérité: Essais de philosophie juridique et morale.* Paris: Dalloz, 1955.

Denning, A. *The Road to Justice.* London: Stevens & Sons, 1955.

Dressner, S. H. *Tsaddik: An Inspired Study of the Mystical Leader of Eighteenth-Century Hasidism.* London: Abelard-Schuman, 1954.

Dünner, A. *Die Gerechtigkeit nach dem Alten Testament.* Bonn: H. Bouvier, 1963.

Eckhoff, T. *Justice: Its Determinants in Social Interaction.* Rotterdam: Rotterdam University Press, 1974.

Ellul, J. *Le fondement théologique du droit.* Neuchâtel: Delachaux & Niestlé, 1946.

Fahlgren, K. H. *Tsedeka, nahestehende und entgegengestellte Begriffe im Alten Testament.* Uppsala: Almquist & Wiksells Boktrykeri, 1932.

Falk, Z. W. *Hebrew Law in Biblical Times.* Jerusalem: Wahrmann Books, 1964.

Frantzen, A. J. *The Literature of Penance in Anglo-Saxon England.* New Brunswick: Rutgers University Press, 1983.

Gorecki, J. *A Theory of Criminal Justice.* New York: Columbia University Press, 1979.

Guiraud, J. *L'inquisition médiévale.* Paris: Librairie Jules Talandier, 1978.

Havelock, E. A. *The Greek Concept of Justice: From Its Shadow in Homer to Its Substance in Plato.* Cambridge: Harvard University Press, 1978

Heath, J. *Eighteenth-Century Penal Theory.* London: Oxford University Press, 1963.

Immink, P. W. A. *La liberté et la peine.* Assen: Van Gorcum, 1973.

Jacobs, L. *Studies in Talmudic Logic and Methodology.* London: Vallentine, Mitchell, 1961.

Jones, A. H. M. *The Criminal Courts of the Roman Republic and Principate.* Oxford: Basil Blackwell, 1972.

Koch, K. *Um das Prinzip der Vergeltung in Religion und Recht des Alten Testaments.* Darmstadt: Wissenschaftliche Buchgesellschafts, 1972.

Kunkel, W. *Kleine Schriften: Zum römischen Strafverfahren und zur römischen Verfassungsgeschichte.* Weimar: Bohlau Verlag, 1974.

Lange, H. *Schadenersatz und Privatstrafe in der mittel alterlichen Rechtstheorie.* Bd. 2, *Forschungen zur neueren Privatrechtsgeschichte.* Munster and Cologne: Bohlau Verlag, 1955.

Levinas, E. *Totalité et infini: Essai sur l'exteriorité.* The Hague: Nijhoff, 1961.

―――. *Difficile liberté: Essai sur le judaïsme.* Paris: Albin Michel, 1963.

Liebs, D. *Die Klagenkonkurrenz im römischen Recht: Zur Geschichte der Scheidung von Schadenersatz und Privatstrafe.* Göttingen: Vandenhoeck & Ruprecht, 1972.

Little, D. *Religion and the Order of Law.* Chicago: University of Chicago Press, 1984.

Lloyd-Jones, H. *The Justice of Zeus.* Berkeley: University of California Press, 1971.

Lyons, D. *Ethics and the Rule of Law.* Cambridge: Cambridge University Press, 1984.

McHugh, G. A. *Christian Faith and Criminal Justice: Toward a Christian Response to Crime and Punishment.* New York: Paulist Press, 1978.

McKenzie, J. G. *Guilt: Its Meaning and Significance.* London: Allen & Unwin, 1962.

Mach, R. *Der Tsaddik in Talmud und Midrash.* Leiden: E. J. Brill, 1957.

Marcus, H. *Metaphysik der Gerechtigkeit.* Basel: Ernst Reinhardt, 1947.

Meurer, S. *Das Recht im Dienst der Versöhnung und des Friedens: Studie zur Frage des Rechts nach dem Neuen Testament.* Zürich: Theologischer Verlag, 1972.

Mommsen, T. *Römisches Strafrecht.* Leipzig: Duncker & Humblot, 1899.

Newman, G. R. *The Punishment Response.* Albany: Harrow & Heston, 1985.

Nicholas, B. *An Introduction to Roman Law.* Oxford: Clarendon Press, 1962.

Oppenheimer, H. *The Rationale of Punishment.* London: University of London Press, 1913.

Pedersen, J. *Israel: Its Life and Culture.* 2 vols. London: Oxford University Press; Copenhagen: Branner, 1940.

Phillips, A. *Ancient Israel's Criminal Law: A New Approach to the Decalogue.* Oxford: Basil Blackwell, 1970.

Powell, C. H. *The Biblical Concept of Power.* London: Epworth Press, 1963.

Rabinowitz, J. J. *Jewish Law: Its Influence on the Development of Legal Institutions.* New York: Bloch, 1956.

Radbruch, G. *Elegantia juris criminalis: Sieben Studien zur Geschichte des Strafrechts.* Basel: Verlag für Recht und Gesellschaft, 1936.

———. *Der Mensch im Recht.* Göttingen: Van den Hoeck & Ruprecht, 1949.

Rawls, J. *A Theory of Justice.* 2d ed. Cambridge: Harvard University Press, 1972.

Reed, W. E., and F. Sand Reed. *Contract with God.* New York: Four Seasons, 1964.

Reik, T. *Myth and Guilt: The Crime and Punishment of Mankind*. London: Hutchinson, 1958.
Rescher, N. *Distributive Justice*. New York: Bobbs-Merrill, 1966.
Rosenthal, E. I. J., ed. *Law and Religion*. Vol. 3 of *Judaism and Christianity*. London: Sheldon Press, 1938.
Santalucia, B. *Diritto e processo penale nell'antica Roma*. Milan: Giufrè, 1989.
Sarano, J. *La culpabilité*. Paris: Librairie Armand Colin, 1957.
Sawer, G. *Law in Society*. Oxford: Clarendon Press, 1965.
Schulz, F. *Principles of Roman Law*. Oxford: Clarendon Press, 1956.
Sellin, J. T. *Slavery and the Penal System*. New York: Elsevier, 1976.
Snaith, N. H. *The Distinctive Ideas of the Old Testament*. London: Epworth Press, 1944.
Stone, J. *Human Law and Human Justice*. Stanford: Stanford University Press, 1965.
Sundin, J. "Control, Punishment and Reconciliation: A Case of Parish Justice in Sweden before 1880." In *Tradition and Transition: Studies in Microdemography and Social Change*, ed. A. Brandström and J. Sundin. Sweden: Demographic Data Base, University of Umeå, 1981.
Tapp, J. L. T., and F. J. Levin. *Law, Justice, and the Individual in Society: Psychological and Legal Issues*. New York: Holt, Rinehart, & Winston, 1977.
Ten, C. L. *Crime, Guilt, and Punishment: A Philosophical Introduction*. Oxford: Clarendon Press, 1987.
Tournier, P. *Vraie ou fausse culpabilité*. Neuchâtel: Delachaux & Niestlé, 1954.
Tresmontant, C. *Essai sur la pensée hébraique*. Paris: Les Editions du Cerf, 1953.
Verdam, P. J. *Mosaic Law in Practice and Study throughout the Ages*. Kampen: Kok, 1959.
Vogel, C. *Le Pécheur et la pénitence dans l'eglise ancienne*. Paris: Les Editions du Cerf, 1982.

## 2. Two Concepts of Law

Becker, H. *Outsiders: Studies in the Sociology of Deviance*. New York: Free Press, 1963.
Bernstein, B. *Class, Codes, and Control*. London: Routledge & Kegan Paul, 1972.
Bianchi, H. *Stigmatisering*. Deventer: Kluwer, 1972.
Clinard, M. B., ed. *Anomie and Deviant Behavior*. New York: Free Press, 1971.

Culhane, C. *Barred from Prison*. Vancouver: Pulp Press, 1981.

Deleuze, G., and F. Guattari. *L'anti-Oedipe*. Paris: Editions de Minuit, 1972.

Douglas, J. D., ed. *Deviance and Respectability: The Social Construction of Moral Meanings*. New York: Basic Books, 1970.

Durkheim, E. *The Elementary Forms of Religious Life*. London: Allen & Unwin, 1915.

————. *Suicide*. London: Routledge & Kegan Paul, 1951.

————. *Professional Ethics and Civic Morals*. London: Routledge & Kegan Paul, 1957.

————. *The Division of Labor in Society*. New York: Free Press, 1964.

————. *The Rules of Sociological Method*. New York: Free Press, 1966.

Finifter, A. W., ed. *Alienation and the Social System*. New York: Wiley, 1972.

Freire, P. *Pedagogy of the Oppressed*. London: Sheed & Ward, 1972.

Gerhardt, U. E., and M. E. J. Wadsworth. *Stress and Stigma: The Dilemma of Explanation in the Sociology of Crime and Illness*. London: Macmillan, 1985.

Ginsberg, R. B. *Anomie and Aspirations: A Reinterpretation of Durkheim's Theory*. New York: Arno Press, 1980.

Goffman, E. *Stigma: Notes on the Management of Spoiled Identity*. Englewood Cliffs, N.J.: Prentice-Hall, 1963.

Hagan, J., ed. *Deterrence Reconsidered: Methodological Innovations*. Beverly Hills: Sage, 1982.

Hirst, P. Q. *Durkheim, Bernard, and Epistemology*. London: Routledge & Kegan Paul, 1975.

Merton, R. K. *Social Theory and Social Structure*. New York: Free Press, 1968.

Orru, M. *Anomie, History, and Meanings*. Boston: Allen & Unwin, 1987.

Packer, H. L. *The Limits of the Criminal Sanction*. Stanford: Stanford University Press, 1973.

Perrot, M., ed. *L'impossible prison*. Paris: Seuil, 1980.

Petit, J. C. *Ces peines obscures: La prison pénale de 1789–1870*. Paris: Seuil, 1990.

Powell, E. H. *The Design of Discord: Studies of Anomie*. New Brunswick: Transaction Books, 1988.

Prichard, H. A. *Moral Obligation*. Oxford: Clarendon Press, 1949.

Sacco, V. F. *Perceptions of Crime and Anomic Adaptations*. Edmonton, Alberta: Population Research Laboratory, University of Alberta, 1984.

Sharp, G. *The Politics of Non-Violent Action*. Boston: Porter Sargent, 1971.

Shoham, S. *The Mark of Cain: The Stigma Theory of Crime and Social Deviation*. Jerusalem: Israel University Press, 1970.

Tocqueville, A. de. *On the Penitentiary System in the United States and Its Application in France* (1832). Carbondale, Ill.: Southern Illinois University Press, 1964.

## 3. The Assensus Model

Abel, R., ed. *The Politics of Informal Justice*. New York: Academic Press, 1982.

Armstrong, T. E. *Japanese Consensus Methods and Their Relevance to Canada*. Kingston, Ontario: Industrial Relations Centre, Queen's University at Kingston, 1988.

Atkinson, D. *Orthodox Consensus and Radical Alternative: A Study in Sociological Theory*. London: Heinemann Educational, 1971.

Aubert, V. "Competition and Dissensus: Two Types of Conflict Resolution." *Journal of Conflict Resolution* 7 (1963): 26–42.

Bau, P. *Exchange of Power in Social Life*. London: Wiley, 1964.

Beran, H. *The Consent Theory of Political Obligation*. London: Croom Helm, 1987.

Bernard, T. J. *The Consensus-Conflict Debate: Form and Content in Social Theories*. New York: Columbia University Press, 1983.

Center for the Study of Democractic Institutions. *Natural Law and Modern Society*. Cleveland: World, 1963.

Clastres, P. *La société contre l'état*. Paris: Editions de Minuit, 1974.

Franks, C. E. S. *Dissent and the State*. Toronto: Oxford University Press, 1989.

Gurvitch, G. *Dialectique et sociologie*. Paris: Presses Universitaires de France, 1962.

Herzog, D. *Happy Slaves: A Critique of Consent Theory*. Chicago: University of Chicago Press, 1989.

Hodges, H. *Conflict and Consensus: An Introduction to Sociology*. New York: Harper & Row, 1971.

Le Goff, J., and P. Nora. *Faire l'histoire*. 3 vols. Paris: Gallimard, 1974.

Lipset, S. M. *Consensus and Conflict: Essays in Political Sociology*. New Brunswick: Transaction Books, 1985.

Partridge, P. *Consent and Consensus*. New York: Macmillan, 1970.

Pepin, J. *Saint Augustin et la dialectique*. Villanova, Pa.: Augustinian Institute, Villanova University, 1976.

Pepinsky, H. *Crime and Conflict: A Study of Law and Society*. London: Martin Robertson, 1976.

———. *Crime Control Strategies: An Introduction to the Study of Crime*. New York: Oxford University Press, 1980.

———. *The Geometry of Violence and Democracy.* Bloomington: Indiana University Press, 1991.

Quinney, R. *The Problem of Crime: A Critical Introduction to Criminology.* New York: Harper, 1977.

Roodenburg, H. *Onder censuur: De kerkelijke tucht in de gereformeerde gemeente van Amsterdam, 1578–1700.* Hilversum: Verloren, 1990.

Rossi, I. *From the Sociology of Symbols to the Sociology of Signs: Toward a Dialectical Sociology.* New York: Columbia University Press, 1983.

Sandywell, B., et al. *Problems of Reflexivity and Dialectics in Sociological Inquiry.* London: Routledge & Kegan Paul, 1975.

Siegrist, J. *Das Consensus-Modell: Studien zur Interaktions theorie und zur kognitiven Sozialisation.* Stuttgart: Ferdinand Enke, 1970.

Taylor, I., P. Walton, and J. Young. *The New Criminology: For a Social Theory of Deviance.* London: Routledge & Kegan Paul, 1973.

Taylor, I., P. Walton, and J. Young, eds. *Critical Criminology.* London: Routledge & Kegan Paul, 1975.

Wheeler, H., ed. *Beyond the Punitive Society: Operant Conditioning, Social and Political Aspects.* San Francisco: W. H. Freeman, 1973.

## 4. Dispute Settlement

Abel, C. F., and F. H. Marsh. *Punishment and Restitution.* Westport, Conn.: Greenwood Press, 1984.

Alper, B. S. *Prisons Inside-Out: Alternatives in Correctional Reform.* Cambridge: Ballinger, 1974.

Alper, B. S., and L. Nichols. *Beyond the Courtroom: Programs in Community Justice and Conflict Resolution.* Lexington, Mass.: Lexington Books, 1981.

Amernic, J. *Victims: The Orphans of Justice.* Toronto: McClelland and Stewart-Bantam, 1984.

Archibald, K., ed. *Strategic Interaction and Conflict.* Berkeley: Institute of International Studies, University of California, 1966.

Argyle, M. *Social Interaction.* London: Tavistock, 1973.

Berger, P., and T. Luckman. *The Social Construction of Reality.* Garden City, N.Y.: Doubleday, 1966.

Blad, J. R., H. v. Mastrigt, and N. A. Uildriks, eds. *The Criminal Justice System as a Social Problem: An Abolitionist Perspective.* Rotterdam: Erasmus University Press, 1987.

Bossy, J. *Disputes and Settlements: Law and Human Relations in the West.* Cambridge: Cambridge University Press, 1983.

Boulding, K. *Conflict and Defense: A General Theory.* New York: Harper, 1962.

Briggs, D. *In Place of Prisons*. London: Maurice Temple Smith, 1975.

Burton, J. W. *Conflict: Resolution and Prevention*. Basingstoke: Macmillan, 1990.

Campbell, R. *Justice through Restitution*. Milford, Mich.: Mott Media, 1977.

Caplow, T. *Two against One*. Englewood Cliffs, N.J.: Prentice-Hall, 1968.

Clegg, S. *Power, Rule and Domination: A Critical and Empirical Understanding of Power in Sociological Theory and Organization Life*. London: Routledge & Kegan Paul, 1975.

Conklin, J. E. *The Impact of Crime*. New York: Macmillan, 1975.

Coser, L. A. *The Functions of Social Conflict*. Glencoe, Ill.: Free Press, 1975.

Deutsch, M. *Resolution of Conflict*. New Haven, Conn.: Yale University Press, 1974.

Ellickson, R. C. *Order without Law: How Neighbors Settle Disputes*. Cambridge: Harvard University Press, 1991.

Etzioni, A. *Complex Organizations*. New York: Free Press, 1971.

Festinger, L. *Conflict, Decision, and Dissonance*. Stanford: Stanford University Press, 1964.

Folberg, J., and A. Taylor. *Mediation: A Comprehensive Guide to Resolving Conflicts without Litigation*. San Francisco: Jossey-Bass, 1984.

Freedman, L., et al. *Confidentiality in Mediation: A Practitioner's Guide*. Chicago: ABA, 1985.

Gibbs, J. L. "The K'pelle Moot: A Therapeutic Model for the Informal Settlement of Disputes." *Africa* 33 (1963).

Goffman, E. *The Presentation of Self in Everyday Life*. New York: Doubleday Anchor Books, 1959.

———. *Encounters: Two Studies in the Sociology of Interaction*. Indianapolis: Bobbs-Merrill, 1961.

———. *Behavior in Public Places: Notes on the Social Organization of Gatherings*. New York: Free Press, 1963.

———. *Interaction Ritual: Essays on Face-to-Face Behavior*. Chicago: Aldine, 1967.

———. *Strategic Interaction*. Oxford: Basil Blackwell, 1970.

Goldberg, S. B., et al. *Dispute Resolution*. Boston: Little, Brown, 1985.

Gulliver, P. H. *Disputes and Negotiations: A Cross-Cultural Perspective*. New York: Academic Press, 1979.

Haan, W. de. *The Politics of Redress: Crime, Punishment, and Abolition*. London: Unwin & Hyman, 1990.

Hagan, J. *Victims before the Law*. Toronto: Butterworth, 1983.

Hardin, J. *Victims and Offenders*. London: Bedford Square Press, 1982.

Harrington, C. B. *Shadow Justice: The Ideology and Institutionalization of Alternatives to Court.* Westport, Conn.: Greenwood Press, 1985.

Hudson, J., and B. Galaway, eds. *Considering the Victim: Readings in Restitution and Victim Compensation.* Springfield, Ill.: Thomas, 1975.

————. *Offender Restitution in Theory and Action.* Lexington, Mass.: D. C. Heath, 1977.

————. *Restitution in Criminal Justice: A Critical Assessment of Sanctions.* Lexington, Mass.: Lexington Books, 1977.

————. *Victims, Offenders, and Alternative Sanctions.* Lexington, Mass.: Lexington Books, 1978.

————. *Perspectives on Crime Victims.* Toronto: C. V. Mosby, 1981.

Kagel, S., and K. Kelley. *The Anatomy of Mediation: What Makes It Work.* Washington, D.C.: Bureau of National Affairs, 1989.

Kanowitz, L. *Cases and Materials on Alternative Dispute Resolution.* St. Paul, Minn.: West, 1985.

Kittrie, N. N. *The Right To Be Different: Deviance and Enforced Therapy.* Baltimore: Johns Hopkins University Press, 1971.

McDonald, W. F. *Criminal Justice and the Victim.* Beverly Hills: Sage, 1976.

McNeil, E. *The Nature of Human Conflict.* Englewood Cliffs, N.J.: Prentice-Hall, 1965.

Marshall, T. F. *Alternatives to Criminal Courts: The Potential for Non-Judicial Dispute Settlement.* Aldershot, Hampshire: Gower, 1985.

Meiners, R. E. *Victim Compensation.* Lexington, Mass.: D. C. Heath, 1978.

Merry, S. E. *Getting Justice and Getting Even: Legal Consciousness among Working Class Americans.* Chicago: University of Chicago Press, 1990.

Miller, S. M., and P. Roby. *The Future of Inequality.* New York: Basic Books, 1970.

Nettler, G. *Responding to Crime.* Ohio: Anderson, 1982.

Rainwater, Lee. *Social Problems and Policy: Inequality and Justice.* Chicago: Aldine, 1974.

Rapoport, A. *Fights, Games, and Debates.* Ann Arbor: University of Michigan Press, 1960.

————. *Two-Person Game Theory: The Essential Ideas.* Ann Arbor: University of Michigan Press, 1966.

Rapoport, A., and A. Chammah. *The Prisoner's Dilemma: A Study in Conflict and Cooperation.* Ann Arbor: University of Michigan Press, 1965.

Ray, L. *Alternative Dispute Resolution.* Washington, D.C.: American Bar Association, 1982.

Reid, J. P. *A Law of Blood: The Primitive Law of the Cherokee Nation.* New York: New York University Press, 1970.

Sander, F. E. A. *Mediation: A Select Annotated Bibliography.* Washington, D.C.: American Bar Association, 1979.

Schafer, S. *Compensation and Restitution to Victims of Crime.* Patterson Smith, 1970.

————. *Victimology.* Reston, Va.: Reston, 1977.

Schelling, T. C. *The Strategy of Conflict.* Cambridge: Harvard University Press, 1963.

Schneider, H. J., ed. *The Victim in International Perspective.* New York: Walter de Gruyter, 1982.

Shonholtz, R. "A New Justice Theory and Practice." In H. Bianchi and R. v. Swaaningen, *Abolitionism.*

Shubik, M. *Games for Society, Business, and War.* New York: Elsevier, 1975.

Simkin, W. E. *Mediation and the Dynamics of Collective Bargaining.* Washington, D.C.: Bureau of National Affairs, 1971.

Skolnick, J. H. *Justice without Trial: Law Enforcement in a Democratic Society.* New York: Wiley, 1967.

Society of Professionals in Dispute Resolution. *Ethical Issues in Dispute Resolution.* Washington, D.C.: American Arbitrary Association, 1984.

Swingle, P., ed. *The Structure of Conflict.* New York: Academic Press, 1970.

Thomas, D. K. *Dispute Resolution from an Anthropological Perspective.* Washington, D.C.: Society of Professionals in Dispute Resolution, 1984.

Walton, R. E. *Interpersonal Peacemaking, Confrontation, and Third Party Consultation.* Reading, Mass.: Addison Wesley, 1969.

Wright, M. *Making Good.* London: Burnett Books, 1982.

## 5. Sanctuary

Behaghel, J. W. *Disquisitio politico-juridica an et quatenus asyla in republica Christiana sint toleranda.* Utrecht, 1748.

Bohannan, P. *Law and Warfare: Studies in the Anthropology of Conflict.* Garden City, N.Y.: Doubleday, 1967.

Cauwenbergh, E. v. *Les pélérinages expiatoires et judiciaires dans le droit communal de la Belgique au moyen âge.* Louvain: Bureaux de Recueil, 1922.

Chan, J. B. L., and R. V. Ericson. *Decarceration and the Economy of Penal Reform*. Toronto: University of Toronto Press, 1981.

Christie, N. *Limits of Pain*. Oslo: Universitets Forlag, 1981.

Cox, J. C. *The Sanctuaries and Sanctuary Seekers in Medieval England*. London: George Allen, 1911.

Crittenden, A. *Sanctuary*. New York: Weidenfeld & Nicolson, 1988.

Dodge, C. R. *A World without Prisons*. Lexington, Mass.: D. C. Heath, 1979.

Gijswijt Hofstra, M. *Wijkplaatsen voor vervolgden: Asielverlening in Culemborg, Vianen, Buren, Leerdam, en Ijsselstein van de 16e tot eind 18e eeuw*. Dieren: Bataafsche Leeuw, 1984.

Inciardi, J. A., A. A. Block, and L. A. Hallowell. *Historical Approaches to Crime*. Beverly Hills: Sage, 1977.

MacEoin, G., ed. *Sanctuary: A Resource Guide for Understanding and Participating in the Central American Refugee's Struggle*. San Francisco: Harper & Row, 1985.

McDaniel, J. *Sanctuary*. Ithaca, N.Y.: Cornell University Press, 1987.

Martin, D. A., ed. *The New Asylum Seekers: Refuge Law in the 1980s*. Dordrecht: Martinus Nijhoff, 1988.

Oeveren, B. v. *De Vrijsteden in het Oude Testament*. Kampen: Kok, 1968.

Riggs, C. H. *Criminal Asylum in Anglo-Saxon Law*. Gainesville: University of Florida Press, 1963.

Scheffer, J., ed. *Sanctuary and Asylum: A Handbook for Commitment*. Geneva: Studies from the World Alliance of Reformed Churches, 1990.

Sordi, M., ed. *I santuari e la guerra nel mondo classico*. Milan: Vita e Pensiero, 1984.

Stanley, S., and M. Baginsky. *Alternatives to Prisons*. London: Peter Owen, 1984.

Tomsho, R. *The American Sanctuary Movement*. Austin: Texas Monthly Press, 1987.

Verdier, R. *La vengeance: Etudes d'ethnologie, d'histoire et de philosophie*. Paris: Editions Cujas, 1980.

## 6. Strategies of Change

Bauman, Z. *Towards a Critical Sociology: An Essay on Common Sense and Emancipation*. London: Routledge & Kegan Paul, 1976.

Bianchi, J. "Pitfalls and the Strategy of Abolition." Opening address to the Second International Conference on Penal Abolition in Amsterdam, 1985. In R. v. Swaaningen et al., *A tort et a travers:*

*Liber amicorum Herman Bianchi.* Amsterdam: Free University Press, 1986.

Bloch, E. *Das Prinzip Hoffnung.* 3 vols. Frankfurt on Main: Suhrkamp, 1959.

Jordan, N. *Themes in Speculative Psychology.* London: Tavistock, 1968.

Menninger, K. *The Crime of Punishment.* 2d ed. New York: Viking Press, 1968.

Moltmann, J. *Hope and Planning.* New York: Harper & Row, 1971.

# INDEX

Herman Bianchi is retired Professor of Criminology and former Dean of the Law School of the Free University in Amsterdam.